healthy
baby & toddler
foods

mitchell beazley

healthy
baby & toddler
foods

the complete healthy diet for
0 to 3-year-olds

amanda grant

Healthy Baby & Toddler Foods
by Amanda Grant

Healthy Baby & Toddler Foods is meant to be used as a general reference and recipe book. While the author believes the information and recipes it contains are beneficial to health, the book is in no way intended to replace medical advice. You are therefore urged to consult your health-care professional about specific medical issues or complaints.

First published in Great Britain in 2001 as *Organic Baby and Toddler Foods* by Mitchell Beazley, an imprint of Octopus Publishing Group Limited, 2–4 Heron Quays, London E14 4JP.
© Octopus Publishing Group Limited 2001
Text © Amanda Grant 2001
Reissued 2004

ISBN 1 84000 938 1

Commissioning Editor: Rebecca Spry
Executive Art Editor: Phil Ormerod
Managing Editor: Emma Rice
Design: Miranda Harvey
Editor: Jo Richardson
Proofreader: Jamie Ambrose
Counsultant Nutritionist: Tanya Carr
Production: Alix McCulloch
Index: John Noble

Typeset in Helvetica Neue
Printed and bound by Toppan Printing Company in China

contents

these symbols are used in the recipe sections:

❄ suitable for freezing

 also suitable for babies

 also suitable for toddlers

⏱ prepare in advance

nutritional units of measurement

g	gram	
mg	milligram	one thousandth of 1 g
mcg	microgram	one-millionth of 1 g
ng	nanogram	one-thousand-millionth of 1 g
kg	kilogram	1,000 g
kcal	kilocalorie	1 calorie (unit used to measure the energy value of food)

Good nutrition for your baby or toddler is vital to help her body to function, repair itself, and grow efficiently, and to ensure good health throughout life. This means eating a healthy, well-balanced diet, rich in energy and nutrients.

Because young children's requirements for energy and nutrients are high but their appetites are low, you need to make sure that meals are small, frequent, and made up of "nutrient-dense" foods. All foods provide a mixture of nutrients, but no single food provides them all, so your child's diet needs to be varied. Introduce a wide range of flavours and textures of fresh, unrefined, preferably organic foods, largely free from potentially harmful chemical residues, as early as possible.

Most healthy-eating guidelines for adults recommend low-fat, high-fibre diets, but this is not suitable for young children. They need fat for energy, and too much fibre will put stress on their immature digestive systems. Nevertheless, a healthy family lifestyle will encourage toddlers to eat more healthily; feed them the same as the rest of the family by the time they are five years old at the latest.

From the moment babies start breast-feeding they learn that eating is a pleasurable experience. It is important to build on this and to remember that your attitude to food will be the main influence on your child's diet.

Try to encourage your child to like food. Don't assume, for example, that she will instinctively hate vegetables and love sweet things. Ella, my eldest daughter, loves vegetables, mostly because we eat them with her and have never given her a reason not to like them. Ultimately, healthy eating should be something your child sees as fun.

baby & toddler nutrition

a baby's nutrients

energy

Babies and toddlers need energy for growth, development, and general health. For their size, children have high energy requirements. These increase quickly because they are growing fast and becoming more active. It is beneficial to your child's health to encourage an increase in energy expenditure: early interest in exercise sets up good standards.

sources

The main sources of energy in our diet are carbohydrates, protein, and fat. The amount of energy made available by each source varies. Fat is the most concentrated source – weight for weight, it provides just over twice as much as either protein or carbohydrates. However, it is far better to give babies and toddlers foods that are not only energy-rich but also high in essential nutrients: avocados, bananas, nut butters (but *see* page 33), cheese, and lentils.

carbohydrates

Babies and toddlers need carbohydrates for growth, development, and energy. Getting the right balance is very important, since too little can inhibit their growth and energy levels, but too many – especially refined carbohydrates – can cause dental cavities, obesity, and other health problems.

sources

Sugar, starch, and fibre are the three main types of carbohydrates. Natural sugars from fruit and vegetables and natural starches from wholegrain cereals, breads, brown rice, and potatoes are the best forms, since they release energy slowly.

include food from these groups for a balanced diet

Milk and dairy foods
Include: milk (for specific advice about milk, *see* page 35), yogurt, mascarpone, fromage frais, butter and cheese, e.g. Cheddar and cream cheese.
Provide: protein, vitamin A, vitamin B_{12}, calcium and fat.

Meat, fish and alternatives
Include: meat, fish, poultry, eggs, beans, lentils
Provide: many nutrients including protein, iron, zinc, B vitamins

Breads, other cereals, and potatoes
Include: oats, breakfast cereals, bread, rice, pasta, potatoes, sweet potatoes
Provide: starch for energy, calcium, magnesium, iron, B vitamins, fibre

Fruits and vegetables
Include: apples, pears, mangoes, bananas, broccoli, green beans, peppers, etc.
Provide: a wide range of vitamins and minerals, fibre, and energy.

protein

Babies and toddlers need proteins for healthy growth and development. If energy needs are not met by carbohydrates and fat, dietary protein is used preferentially as a source of energy rather than for tissue growth and repair, so it is important to make sure that your child gets enough. Because babies are growing rapidly, they require proportionately more protein than adults. Breast or formula milk is the major source of protein for the first eight months. Protein-rich foods should then be introduced gradually as breast-feeding decreases: too much protein could strain your baby's kidneys.

sources

Good protein sources include lean meat (especially chicken and lamb), fish, eggs, and cheese. Good protein sources for vegetarians and vegans include cereals, nuts, seeds, and pulses.

protein source	provides
50 g lamb *loin, lean only, grilled*	13.9 g
50 g beef *mince, stewed*	11.5 g
400 ml whole milk, *pasteurized*	12.8 g
25 g cashew nuts	5.12 g
25 g hazelnuts	3.5 g
150 g red lentils, *boiled*	11.4 g
100 g tofu, *steamed*	8.1 g

fats

Babies and toddlers need fat for energy to grow, and also to protect and insulate their vital organs. Fat also enables their bodies to absorb the fat-soluble vitamins A, D, E, and K. While your child's diet shouldn't contain a high proportion of fat (especially saturated fat; *see* below), it is unnecessary to restrict the fat in your child's diet, particularly at under two years of age.

sources

Fats can either be saturated – from foods such as meat and dairy products – or unsaturated: from oils, avocados, oily fish, and nuts. Unsaturated fats also contain essential fatty acids which the body cannot manufacture itself, so it is important to provide these for your baby. Essential fatty acids, which are found in nuts, plant oils, and oily fish, are vital for the development of the brain.

fibre

Babies and toddlers need fibre in small quantities to keep their bowel movements regular. However, children under the age of two should not have too much fibre (found in brown rice, bran, and whole wheat) since their immature digestive systems cannot cope with it. Too much will also inhibit the absorption of some vitamins and minerals – especially iron and calcium.

sources

The best sources of fibre for babies and toddlers are peas, oats, beans, and fresh fruit and vegetables. Bran or foods with added bran, except that found in wholegrain breads and breakfast cereals, should not be given to babies and toddlers.

Constipation is quite a common problem in young children and can usually be treated by increasing the amount of fruit, vegetables, and wholemeal bread in the diet. I found with Ella that pears relieved constipation and bananas made it worse! Speak to your health visitor, GP, or a registered dietician or nutritionist if you are worried about constipation in your child.

vitamins

Vitamins are essential for numerous body functions including brain function, and they also play an important role in preventing disease. Most vitamins cannot be made by the body, so they must be included in your baby's diet. A well-balanced diet should provide all the vitamins your baby needs.

vitamin A

Needed for growth, an efficient immune system to help prevent infections, healthy skin, and good vision. Good sources include milk and other dairy products. Beta-carotene, which the body can convert into vitamin A, is found in carrots and dark-green vegetables such as spinach, broccoli, and watercress.

vitamin C

Needed for good immune-system function, growth, and the formation of collagen – a protein necessary for the development of healthy bones, teeth, and gums. Vitamin C also assists with the absorption of non-haem iron found in, for example, bread and cereals.

Good sources include melon, mangoes, peaches, dried fruit, oranges, sweet potatoes, broccoli, and other green, leafy vegetables.

vitamin D

Needed for the absorption of calcium and the development of a healthy central nervous system. Good food sources include dairy products, canned sardines, tuna, eggs, meat, and fortified foods, e.g. breakfast cereals and margarine.

vitamin A source	provides	vitamin C source	provides	vitamin D source	provides
25 g butter	203 mcg	100 g oranges	54 mg	50 g sardines,	
50 g scrambled eggs,		75 g broccoli, *boiled*	30 mg	*in oil, drained*	75 mcg
made with milk	148 mcg	100 g sweet potato, *boiled*	17 mg	100 g boiled egg	1.75 mcg
50 g cheddar	62 mcg	100 g mango	37 mg		

Nutritional requirements for different age groups

	0-3 months	4-6 months	7-9 months	10-12 months	1-3 years
protein	12.5 g	12.7 g	13.7 g	14.9 g	14.5 g
vitamin A	350 mcg	350 mcg	350 mcg	350 mcg	400 mcg
Vitamin C	25 mg	25 mg	25 mg	25 mg	30 mg
vitamin D	8.5 mcg	8.5 mcg	7 mcg	7 mcg	7 mcg
energy	*boys* 545 *girls* 515	*boys* 690 *girls* 645	*boys* 825 *girls* 765	*boys* 920 *girls* 865	*boys* 1,230 *girls* 1,165
calcium	525 mg	525 mg	525 mg	525 mg	350 mg
iron	1.7 mg	4.3 mg	7.8 mg	7.8 mg	6.9 mg
zinc	4 mg	4 mg	5 mg	5 mg	5 mg

minerals

Minerals are vital for body function. In babies and toddlers they are particularly important for bone and teeth formation and for maintaining a healthy immune system. Eating a varied diet ensures an adequate supply of most minerals.

iron

Babies and toddlers need iron for the formation of haemoglobin in red blood cells. This will prevent iron-deficiency anaemia, often associated with poorer health and slower development. Symptoms are not always obvious: some children continue to run and play; others have a lack of energy and appetite. The body stores of iron that babies are born with tend to be used up when they reach four to six months of age. Milk supplies insufficient iron at this stage of life, so solid foods are needed to ensure good stores.

The most easily absorbed form of iron is haem iron, found in foods of animal origin, e.g. chicken, lamb, and some fish, especially canned sardines and tuna. Non-haem iron is mainly found in foods of plant origin: cereals, pulses, green vegetables, dried fruit, and fortified breakfast cereals. Foods high in vitamin C (see page 10) help the body to absorb iron, so serve these foods together, e.g. freshly squeezed orange juice with a bowl of breakfast cereal topped with chopped dried apricots. This is particularly important for vegetarians and vegans. Tannins in tea and coffee hinder iron absorption, so are best omitted from a child's diet.

calcium

Breast and formula milk contain all the calcium your baby initially needs. Once you reduce milk feeds and start weaning, your child will need more calcium for the development of healthy teeth and bones, nerve functioning, and blood clotting. Good sources of calcium include milk, hard cheeses, canned fish, and green vegetables.

zinc

Babies and toddlers need zinc for healthy development and growth, tissue repair, and a healthy immune system. Good sources of zinc include red meat, sunflower seeds, and peanuts.

supplements

If babies and toddlers are being fed a well-balanced diet and have a good appetite, they shouldn't need any supplements. However, the UK Department of Health advises that children aged six months to five years should be assessed for receiving drops containing vitamins A, C, and D. Drops containing these vitamins should be available from Child Health Centres.

Data in tables: McCance and Widdowson, The Composition of Foods, Fifth Edition.

iron source	provides	calcium source	provides	zinc source	provides
100 g lamb, *lean only grilled*	2.1 mg	50 g hard cheese	335 mg	400 ml milk, *whole pasteurized*	1.6 mg
50 g sardines, *in oil, drained*	1.5 mg	100 g chick-peas, *canned*	43 mg	100 g eggs, *poached*	1.3 mg
100 g sausages, *pork grilled*	1.5 mg	50 g almonds	120 mg	100 g rice, *white, boiled*	0.7 mg
25 g sesame seeds	2.6 mg	25 g sunflower seeds	177 mg	100 g broccoli, *boiled*	0.4 mg
50 g pine nuts	2.8 mg	50 g figs, *dried, ready to eat*	115 mg	75 g dates, *with stones*	0.3 mg

veggie & vegan

Research has shown that a vegetarian diet can still provide all the nutrients necessary for your baby's healthy growth and development.

If your baby is vegetarian or vegan, you will need to pay particular care and attention to the variety and balance of foods that he or she eats. Vegetarians exclude all meat, poultry, and fish from their diet, and sometimes eggs. Nevertheless, nutritional research has shown that a vegetarian diet can still provide all the nutrients necessary for your baby's healthy growth and development.

Vegans exclude all meat, poultry, fish, and dairy products as well as honey from their diets.

Nutritional guidelines for vegans are similar to those for vegetarians. However, because vegetarians gain a number of nutrients from dairy products and eggs, vegans need to ensure that their diets contain plant-food sources of these nutrients. Consequently, you will need to make a little more effort when planning a vegan diet.

breast-feeding

Breast-feeding is particularly important for vegan babies – you should aim to breast-feed for at least the first year. It is also advised that you take a vitamin B_{12} supplement while breast-feeding, since this can be deficient in a vegan's diet. If you decide to bottle-feed, vegan formulas, often soya-based, are available. Riboflavin intakes are also known to be inadequate in vegan diets, and so riboflavin supplementation is usually recomended.

watchpoints

When planning a vegetarian or vegan diet for your baby, apply the same principles of eating a healthy well-balanced diet (see pages 8–9), but pay particular attention to the following.

● **Make sure the diet includes good sources of nutrient-dense energy foods**, e.g. nuts, seeds, and oils.

● **Include good daily sources of iron**, e.g. bread, pulses, green vegetables, and dried fruit. Eggs are also iron-rich.

● **Make sure the diet is high**

in calcium. Dairy produce is the major source for vegetarians. Good vegan sources include tofu, leafy green vegetables, watercress, dried fruit, seeds, nuts, and fortified foods, e.g. bread and soya drinks. Not all soya drinks are fortified, so you should check the label.

● Milk and meat are the primary sources of iodine in the British Diet, and studies have indicated that some vegans may have a low iodine intake. To prevent a deficiency, include good sources such as vegetables, grains, and, if possible, seaweed. Vegans may like to take iodine supplementation in line with the daily recommendations.

● Feed your baby a good variety of protein sources (see page 9).

vitamins

Vegetarians can get vitamin D from eggs and dairy products, while fortified products such as soya milk (which is often fortified with vitamin B_{12}, calcium, and vitamin D) and vegan margarine should be included in a vegan diet.

Vegans need to be aware that their diet can be low in vitamin B_2 (riboflavin) – needed for converting protein, fats, and carbohydrates into energy and for repairing body tissues. Good sources include wholegrains, mushrooms, almonds, leafy green vegetables, and low-salt yeast extracts.

Breast milk provides all the vitamin B_{12} babies need, providing the mother has an adequate intake in her diet. Once solids are introduced, good sources for vegetarians include dairy products and eggs, while good sources for vegans include fortified foods, e.g. some soya drinks, low-salt yeast extract, veggie burgers, breakfast cereals, and vegetable margarine. Check the packaging of individual products to see which are fortified with vitamin B_{12}.

For more information about vegan formulas or vegetarian or vegan diets, contact a state-registered dietician or registered nutritionist, or the Vegetarian or Vegan Societies; see "Useful Addresses", page 139. It is especially important to seek specialist advice if your family has a history of allergies.

Make sure the diet includes good sources of nutrient-dense energy foods, such as nuts, seeds, and oils.

choosing a baby's food

organic

Organic foods must be produced entirely without the use of synthetic pesticides, fungicides, and growth hormones.

The term "organic" doesn't actually refer to the food itself but rather to how it is produced. "Organic" is defined by law, and all organic food production and processing is governed by a strict set of guidelines.

The Soil Association, a UK-based registered charity and organic-certifying body, describes organic farming as a "safe, sustainable farming system, producing healthy crops and livestock without damage to the environment". In fact, the concept of sustainability is at the very core of organic food production: a naturally balanced system doesn't rely on a battery of artificial inputs. Organic foods must be produced entirely without the use of synthetic pesticides, fungicides, fertilizers, and growth hormones, many of which are believed to contribute to the causes of cancer, birth defects, genetic changes, or serious irritation if ingested directly. But more than that, the processing of organic food has to maintain the "integrity" of the food, which means that no added artificial ingredients, preservatives, or irradiation are permitted.

Buying organic, therefore, is a guarantee that your food has been grown and produced according to strict standards, set out in law to prohibit the use of potentially harmful chemicals. These stringent regulations must be followed by the food manufacturers, processors, packers, and importers, as well as the producers and growers.

growing & processing organic foods

Organic farmers rely mainly on crop rotation and natural predators to control diseases, while animal manure and organic compost are used as natural fertilizers.

In the UK, farms wishing to grow organic products are regularly inspected to check that high standards are being maintained. Producers and farmers have to face rigid testing, including soil testing, before organic certification is granted. Currently 70 to 80 per cent of approved producers are certified by the Soil Association (*see* page 138 for more information on certification). It takes a minimum of two years for a farm to gain organic status. During this time, the farm needs to develop natural fertility in the soil and allow pesticide residues to diminish.

Organic farm animals, poultry, and fish are reared in humane, natural environments without the routine use of drugs or antibiotics.

They are fed a varied, natural diet, free from animal-based feed. Residues of hormones and antibiotics that have been found in non-organic meat and fish are suspected of having a detrimental effect on the human immune system.

Organic food is certified free from genetically modified (GM) organisms; if a crop is contaminated with GM, the farm will lose its organic certification. Organic food is also certified free from artificial additives and sweeteners, and it must not be processed with artificial flavourings and colourings.

Organic produce is often picked when fully ripe, is less processed than non-organic foods, and reaches the consumer faster. These factors help to contribute towards a higher nutrient content (by as much as 50 to 100 per cent) than for non-organic equivalents and I have found that very often organic foods have a much better flavour.

Organic fruit and vegetables are not waxed or treated with other additives post-harvest to prolong their shelf-lives. This means that their skins are safer to eat.

labelling organic foods

To check that food is organic, make sure that it carries one of the recognized organic symbols – *see* page 138 for a guide to the various regulatory bodies.

The European Union labelling laws state that:

- Foods labelled "organic" must contain a minimum of 95 per cent organic ingredients (the remaining five per cent must come from approved non-organic sources).
- Foods labelled "made with organic ingredients" must contain a minimum of 70 per cent organic ingredients.
- Processed products that contain less than 70 per cent organic ingredients must not carry the words "organic ingredients" on the label.

pesticides

Despite official limits on the permitted amount of pesticide residues in food, these levels are regularly exceeded.

Pesticides are chemicals designed to kill or damage pests such as insects, weeds, or fungal diseases. Farmers use pesticides to increase their crop yields and therefore help to make cheaper food. However, there is a price to pay, with potential damage to our health and to the environment. Possibly the pesticides that are most harmful to humans are the organophosphates (OPs) and organochlorines (OCs), two families of pesticides used against a wide range of parasites and pests.

While we do not expect to be directly exposed to these chemicals, they can leave residues, which have been detected in a wide variety of foods. These residues are monitored constantly by the UK government. A working party analyzes over 2,300 food samples a year, testing for 85,000 different pesticides. Of the 2,300 samples tested, approximately 60 to 70 are organic (and therefore grown without the use of pesticides). It is extremely rare to find any residues in the organic samples. In fact, in 1999 there was only one reported case: a residue found in an organic apple. Due to the stringent monitoring in organic food production, the apple source was traced back to the farm and it was discovered that the residue had come from a neighbouring non-organic farm. The apple farm was then kept under close scrutiny to make sure that this contamination was prevented from happening again.

Despite official limits on the permitted amount of pesticide residues in food, these levels are reguarly exceeded, as the examples highlighted on the facing page demonstrate.

organic versus non-organic

Some foods have much higher levels of residues than others, particularly imported foods, since regulations overseas are often far less stringent than in the UK. Of particular concern are milk, fruit, and vegetables. The following are some revealing statistics arising from the analysis of non-organic and organic foods.

- **Fruit and vegetable infant foods** – in 1998, 11 per cent of 143 samples of fruit and vegetable infant foods contained residues. Eighteen of these were organic and contained no residues. Multiple residues were found in 10 samples.
- **Fruit and vegetables** – in 1997, 44 per cent of non-organic fruit and vegetables were found to contain pesticide residues, with some exceeding government safety levels. This resulted in the government recommending, for example, that carrots should be topped and peeled before eating to reduce pesticide exposure. Ironically, the skin is where most of the vegetable's valuable nutrients are stored.
- **Chocolate** – in 1998, according to the Soil Association's findings, 75 per cent of samples of chocolates produced in the EU contained residues.
- **Strawberries and oranges** – in 1999, 80 per cent of strawberries had residues, 42 per cent of which were multiple residues. Ninety-four per cent of oranges tested had high numbers of residues, of which 93 per cent had multiple residues. Peeling will reduce the amount of pesticide residue but will not eliminate the risk.
- **Milk** – Ministry of Agriculture studies have revealed lindane residues in a range of British produce. In 1996, over a third of British cow's milk was contaminated with this OC pesticide, related to DDT. It has been banned or heavily restricted in many countries because it has been repeatedly linked to breast cancer. Despite this, lindane has not been fully banned in the UK.
- **Chicken meat and eggs** – in 2001, Richard Young, coordinator of the Soil Association's campaign against the overuse of antibiotics in intensive farming, commented: "Despite repeated assertions by regulators that nearly all poultry products are free from detectable residues, figures show clearly that about 20 per cent of chicken meat and 10 per cent of the eggs tested contain residues of drugs deemed too dangerous for use in human medicine."
- **Beef** – Organochlorines attach themselves to fat. Non-organic cattle are fed with concentrates that may contain fish meal, which is heavy in fat, and therefore may lead to greater exposure to residues. However, organic cattle eat grass, which contains far less fat and is therefore less likely to be exposed to residues.

additives

Food additives come in the form of preservatives, antioxidants, artificial colourings, artificial flavourings, flavour enhancers, artificial sweeteners, stabilizers, and thickeners. In total, there are over 4,000 of these additives.

They each play a different role in factory-produced food. For example, flavour-enhancers (which have little or no flavour of their own) are used to accentuate the natural flavour of foods. Hence, they are often used when very little of a natural ingredient is present.

Thickening agents are natural or chemically modified carbohydrates, which absorb some of the water that is present in food, thereby making the food thicker. Thickening agents also "stabilize" factory-made foods by keeping the complex mixtures of oils, water, acids, and solids well mixed.

most hazardous additives

Although a small number of additives contribute to making some food safe to eat, the majority have no benefit to health. In fact, many additives can cause problems in babies and toddlers. They have been linked to the cause of certain reactions, such as asthma or skin problems, as well as behavioural changes, birth deformities, and even possibly cancer. Very few are known to be completely safe.

This is a concern when you also consider that the quantity of additives that we are consuming today is large. According to the Food Commission, by the time children have reached the age of 17, they are each likely to have consumed their own weight in food additives.

The additives that have been approved for use in food throughout the EU and passed safety testing have been allocated an "E" (European) number. So far, there are 927 approved E-numbers. There are many other ingredients that have not yet been researched fully; these do not have an E-number attached to them, but they can still be used in foods.

Baby foods are covered by special legislation. Thankfully, E-numbers have been banned from use in baby and toddler foods. However, you need to be aware that they can be present in family foods which you may feed to a toddler. Preservatives, colourings, and added salt are also forbidden, because babies are not able to process them.

By the time children have reached the age of 17, they are likely to have consumed their weight in food additives.

genetically modified (GM) foods

Apart from the increasing toll that intensive agriculture is already taking on the environment, there is now a new threat to wildlife from genetically modified (GM) crops. These crops have genes from other species inserted into their genetic make-up in order to give them new properties. The most common property introduced is resistance to herbicides or weedkillers – products that are made by the same companies as the seeds. One company, Monsanto, has engineered a soya bean which is resistant to its herbicide, Round-Up. This practice perpetuates our dependence on chemical herbicides, which kill off many arable weeds, in turn wiping out seed-eating and insect-eating wild birds such as skylarks and blackbirds, and mammals such as dormice.

most hazardous GM foods

The long-term effects of genetic modification on either wildlife or humans are not really known. Since the technology requires the use of antibiotic-resistant genes, there is concern that their ingestion will increase antibiotic resistance in people.

food purity & your baby

Although pesticides have been used for many years, we still don't know the health impact of long-term exposure to them. Nor do we know whether the existing safety levels for pesticide (especially multiple pesticide) residues in food are set low enough, especially for babies and toddlers. Babies and toddlers are at high risk because their bodies are still developing and their organs are immature.

For their small size, babies and toddlers take in a relatively large quantity of food and fluid, which makes them even more vulnerable to the heavy exposure to these chemicals, additives, and GM foods. A baby's digestive system is more efficient at absorbing foods than that of an adult. This enables nutrients to be used more quickly but also makes the baby more vulnerable to toxins. In addition, a baby's immature kidneys are not as proficient at excreting harmful substances, so they circulate in the body for longer. Although research has been carried out on adults, very little has been undertaken on babies and toddlers, so the real effect that these chemicals have on their bodies is still unknown.

why cook?

Preparing and cooking fresh food yourself can maximize your baby's intake of essential nutrients.

Fresh, homemade food made using quality, preferably organic ingredients is the best choice for your baby's health and future. There are many reasons for this:

● **Preparing and cooking fresh food yourself can maximize your baby's intake of essential nutrients** – especially if it is served raw where appropriate or cooked for the shortest possible time.

● **Buying locally produced food when it is in season, cultivated in healthy, fertile soil will help the environment** in which your children are going to grow up.

● **Fresh foods are very likely to look, smell, and taste better than food from jars.** This will help your baby develop an appreciation for fresh, unprocessed foods which will last throughout his or her life. Some research has also shown that your baby is less likely to become a fussy eater if introduced to a wide range of tastes and textures from a young age.

● **Your baby could become used to the smoother texture of pre-bottled food** and therefore find it harder to accept the courser texture of homemade purées.

Even the best pre-bottled organic baby and toddler foods have inevitably lost some of their nutritive values in the processing.

● **It is easier to feed your baby the same food as the rest of the family** if you are making it yourself.
● **Pre-bottled food is the "fast food" or "convenience food" of the baby world.** It is not, as many producers would have us believe, in any way superior to the homemade equivalent. Even the best pre-bottled organic baby and toddler foods have been processed, cooked, and packaged in a factory, and have inevitably lost some of their nutritive values in the processing.

check the label

Look out for the following:
● **Sugars, including dextrose, glucose, fructose, lactose, maltose, honey, and fruit syrups** (if these have been added, it is often a indicator of the fact that not enough high-quality ingredients, e.g. fruit, are included).
● **Meat or vegetable extracts,** hydrolyzed vegetable protein, or yeast in savoury foods, which could indicate over-processing.
● **Flavourings** – these are unnecessary in baby foods and introduce your child to artificial tastes.
● **Processed starches,** including modified cornflour, maltodextrin, rice starch, and wheat starch. These often accompany the overuse of water; they are low-nutrient fillers that dull the flavour of food and take up the space of more nutritious ingredients.

If and when you use pre-bottled foods, add some fresh food, e.g. a mashed banana or grated apple mixed with a jar of fruit purée, will increase the nutritional value of the bottled food.

The delicate physiology of babies and toddlers makes them susceptible to potentially harmful substances in food. Their immature immune and central nervous systems leave them particularly vulnerable to damage from additives, pesticides, and other chemical residues.

Research has found that babies and toddlers have a greater exposure to these substances than adults. This is because, proportionately, they eat larger quantities of a small range of foods, many of which, if non-organic, tend to have the highest residue levels, such as apples and milk.

healthy foods

buying organic foods

Organic produce is one of the fastest-growing areas of food production. There are large organic sections in most supermarkets, and the range of products available is expanding almost daily – especially for babies and toddlers. Large, independent organic supermarkets are also on the increase. Other growth areas include farmers' markets, organic box and mail-order schemes where the food is delivered to your door, and internet-based suppliers.

saving money

The higher cost of organic foods is still a deterrent to some. If cost is an issue:

- **Identify a small group of foods that appear most regularly on your shopping list and choose organic versions.** Staple foods for babies and toddlers include milk (formula or cow's), fruit, vegetables, rice, and pasta.
- **Choose seasonal fruit and vegetables**; they are generally cheaper than out-of-season produce. Buy them in bulk and freeze.
- **Recognize that most processed convenience foods** aimed specifically at children are often more expensive than fresh organic ingredients.
- **Look for frozen organic fruit and vegetables**, which are often cheaper than fresh.

choosing fruit & veg

Bear in mind the following points when choosing fruit and vegetables:

- **Fresh organic fruits and vegetables are less likely to be uniform in colour, shape, and size than their non-organic equivalents.** This doesn't mean that they are inferior; odd shapes and small blemishes are perfectly natural. Just avoid bruised or over-ripe produce.
- **Smell fresh fruit and vegetables** – it is one of the best ways to judge their quality.
- **Slightly muddy vegetables are fine** and don't need to be washed until you come to use them, but (obviously) remove any slugs or caterpillars immediately.
- **Try to buy direct from producers** – at farmers' markets, for example – because you will then get the freshest produce. Markets and farm shops are also a great way of teaching your toddler about food and where it comes from, without all the distractions of supermarkets in the form of multicoloured packets of sweets.

storing organic foods

If you choose organic food, it is generally more perishable than non-organic, since it has no additives or preservatives to prolong its shelf-life. Fruit and vegetables should be handled especially carefully because they can bruise easily.

fridge

All perishable foods should be kept in the fridge. Raw meat and fish must be covered and kept separate from cooked foods. Avoid using plastic clingfilm, since plastic softeners can contaminate food. Invest instead in some airtight containers with lids. They are safer and cheaper in the long run.

Good baby and toddler foods to keep in the fridge include full-fat milk, cheese, salad, fresh fruit juice, yogurt, nuts, nut butters, and seeds.

freezer

Use your freezer to keep a supply of homemade meals at the ready. You can freeze many of the dishes in this book. Frozen fruit and vegetables are also excellent stand-bys. Freezing may reduce their vitamin content, but this is minimal, especially since most are picked and frozen immediately, which helps to preserve their nutrients. Good baby and toddler foods to keep in the freezer include bags of mixed berries, apple purée (freeze purées in ice-cube trays), bread – especially baby pitta breads – and fish.

store-cupboard ingredients

Keep rotating foods on a "first in, first out" basis. Good baby and toddler store-cupboard foods include canned fish, baby rice and brown rice, baby pasta, soya drinks, oats, dried fruit, olive oil, canned tomatoes, and unsalted rice cakes and bread sticks.

Onions, shallots, and garlic can be tied in bunches and hung in the garage, larder, or any cool, airy place; they will last for months. Orchard fruit, such as apples and pears, and root vegetables also last well if stored in a cool, dark place – light will reduce their vitamin content. Routinely remove any that go off to prevent them spoiling the others, and make sure the air can circulate around them.

Use your freezer to keep a supply of homemade meals at the ready. You can freeze many of the dishes in this book.

food preparation & cooking

Wherever possible, steam vegetables instead of boiling them; this maximizes their nutrient content and flavour.

It is important to invest some time and care in food preparation.

- **Always wash your hands thoroughly before preparing food.** Make sure all cooking utensils are washed and thoroughly rinsed free of any detergents. Cook using stainless-steel saucepans and tools, all of which should have been thoroughly cleaned and rinsed. Avoid non-stick pans; they are coated in plastic which can contaminate food.

- **It is a good idea to prepare fresh fruit and vegetables as close to meal times as possible,** since exposure to oxygen destroys vital nutrients. If you are making meals ahead, prepare enough food to last for a maximum of two days when stored in the fridge.

- **Wherever possible, steam vegetables instead of boiling them** in water; this maximizes their nutrient content and flavour. Otherwise, retain vegetable cooking water: it's great to add to sauces, purées, soups, and stocks.

- **Keep vegetable cooking times to a minimum.** Vegetables should not be cooked to a soft pulp but should still have a slight crunch. Frozen vegetables can be cooked without thawing first.

- **Avoid using microwave ovens.** Many scientists are concerned about the effects of microwave radiation on food and its ability to destroy vital nutrients. Of particular importance is the ability of microwaves to destroy breast milk's disease-fighting capabilities. Steaming, baking, and boiling are all preferable cooking methods to microwaving.

- **Remember not to add salt to vegetable cooking water.**

baby kitchen

organic detergents

Many cleaning products used in the kitchen, such as washing-up liquid, are labelled "irritant". Try house products that are mild and will not irritate when they come into contact with your child's skin.

wood

Wood is one of the best materials for kitchen utensils and chopping boards because it has natural antibacterial properties. Invest in a good-quality wooden chopping board and a few spoons, and they should last a lifetime.

hand-held blender

If you only invest in one appliance, this has to be it! Hand-held blenders are great for making purées, soups, and smoothies, with minimal mess. The blender can also travel with you.

juicer

Juicers are brilliant for making fresh, nutritious vegetable and fruit juices. Food processors often have juicing components available as an extra, which means that you don't always need to buy another appliance.

food processor or blender

Shakes, smoothies, and soups can be made in a flash with one of these. There are now small ones on the market especially designed for processing baby foods. (My favourite blender is the Baby Magimix.) Alternatively, a small coffee grinder is very handy for grinding small quantities of muesli, nuts, and seeds.

water filter

The best sort are those that are plumbed in; otherwise Brita makes good ones that fit in the fridge. Just make sure you change the filter regularly.

rubber ice-cube trays

These are fantastic for freezing baby food in small quantities. They are also good for making mini-ices – *see* the recipe for frozen yogurts, page 122. Once frozen, the cubes can then be stored in freezer bags.

airtight containers & plastic zip-lock bags

These are invaluable for storing foods in the fridge and store-cupboard. They make storing, freezing, or transporting any type of food much easier and help to keep it fresh.

steamer

Steamers are readily available in supermarkets, department stores, and cook shops, and offer a quick, easy, and healthy way to cook vegetables. Try to find a bamboo one – often available in oriental supermarkets. A good alternative is to use a metal colander or sieve on top of a wide saucepan, covered with a lid.

Hand-held blenders are great for making purées, soups, and smoothies, with minimal mess.

Breast milk is the perfect food for your baby, and you should aim to continue breast-feeding for at least a year. You may not realize that breast-fed babies have quite a varied diet, since what you eat will affect the flavour and composition of your milk.

Breast milk...
- contains all the nutrients needed for your baby's healthy development and growth during the first few months of life;
- contains special proteins, antibodies, and white blood cells (which cannot be copied in formulas), which help to protect your baby against infection, illness, and disease;
- reduces the risk of your baby developing allergies if there is a family history of allergy;
- helps to prevent constipation;
- is easy for your baby to digest;
- has long-term health benefits – for example, strong teeth and good eyesight;
- helps to build a strong emotional bond between you and your baby. In addition, breast-fed babies can be easier to wean, because they have already tasted traces of what you have eaten in your breast milk.

During their first six months, babies develop quickly. Their birth-weights are likely to double, and they will need more than just breast milk to sustain this growth. At between four and six months of age, you need to continue with milk-feeds, but also start the weaning process by introducing thicker liquids in the form of puréed fruit and vegetables. Foods with more texture can gradually be introduced. This will encourage your baby to chew and swallow. At five months, a baby can reach for objects and should be encouraged to hold food and spoons.

4-8 months

Breast-feeding is definitely best for your baby for at least the first four to six months after birth. It also has many advantages for you.

Breast milk is designed to feed your baby with all the essential nutrients needed for healthy development and growth. Breast-feeding is definitely best for your baby for at least the first four to six months after birth.

benefits to mums

Breast-feeding also has many advantages for mothers.

- **Straight after birth, it causes the pituitary gland to release oxytocin**, the hormone that causes the uterus to contract and expel the placenta, and helps to keep bleeding to a minimum.
- **It reduces the risk of pre-menopausal breast cancer**, ovarian cancer, and fractures from osteoporosis.
- **It helps to increase your metabolism** slightly, which can help you to lose weight after you have given birth.

Your diet

To help make breast-feeding a success for both you and your baby, you need to eat a good, balanced diet. It should include foods from all of the main food groups to provide all the essential nutrients and to avoid dietary deficiency or imbalance.

- **You need to eat plenty of foods rich in starch and fibre** – bread, cereals, and potatoes – to help provide you with energy.
- **You are advised to eat a mixture of five portions of fruit and vegetables a day.** This is much easier than it may first appear.
- **You need to include some milk and dairy produce**, but these need to be eaten in moderation.

breast-feeding

• **Make sure you incorporate some fresh meat and fish** (especially oily fish) or their alternatives, such as tofu, into your diet.

• **You need some fat in your diet**, but be sure to eat more of the unsaturated fats, e.g. olive oil, avocados, and nuts, and less of the saturated fats, e.g. butter and meat.

• **Try to avoid sugary foods and drinks**, or have them only as occasional treats.

The UK Department of Health recommends that you increase the intake of certain vitamins and minerals while you are breast-feeding. Vitamin D supplementation of 10 mcg per day is recommended. For more information about diet during breast-feeding, *see* my book *Healthy Eating for Pregnancy* (£10.99, Mitchell Beazley).

Research indicates that human breast milk can contain pesticide residues and other harmful by-products of intensive farming, which are passed through breast milk to your baby. Therefore you may wish to eat an organic diet when breast-feeding.

It is also a good idea to eat small, frequent meals and snacks. Take time to enjoy your food: eating should be a pleasure. Keep your intake of alcohol low and avoid drinking shortly before a feed, since it can unsettle your baby. You also need to drink lots of water – aim for at least two litres a day – and avoid drinking too much strong tea or coffee.

Finally, try not to restrict your diet. If you are concerned that certain foods may be upsetting your baby, then you may find it helpful to contact La Leche League, The National Childbirth Trust, The Association of Breast-feeding Mothers (*see* "Useful Addresses", page 139), or a state-registered dietician or registered nutritionist.

Remember that, initially, weaning is more of a learning process than a significant source of nutrition. It is an exploration.

For the first four to six months of life, breast milk is all that is needed to supply your baby with adequate nutrition. As early as possible, you can offer your baby cooled boiled water. This will accustom him or her to the taste of water, a drink vital to health. After four months, a baby's energy level grows and more than just milk is needed to meet nutritional needs. It is now that you can continue to feed the same amount of milk, but also introduce thicker liquids in the form of puréed fruit and vegetables. This will also encourage your baby to start to swallow, which, unlike suckling, is not a natural reflex.

This is the best time to begin weaning. It is advisable not to start earlier, since your baby's digestive system is not able to cope with complex foods. Weaning too early will also increase the risk of

allergies later in life; protective factors and the immune system, which help prevent allergies, are not sufficiently developed in children under four months. It is not advisable to start later because milk alone will no longer provide enough nutrients.

Signs to look out for

There are many signs which indicate that your baby is ready for weaning. These may include being hungry after a big breast- or bottle-feed, drooling or crying when seeing food, chewing on everything in sight, less time in between feeds, or becoming more unsettled at night. Remember that, initially, weaning is more of a learning process than a significant source of nutrition. It is an exploration.

First foods should be simple and of just one flavour, so that they will

weaning
4–6 months

appeal more easily to your baby's as yet undeveloped sense of taste. Baby rice mixed with breast milk or formula is a good first food, since it is bland and easy to digest. A little later on, introduce puréed apple, carrot, potato, or banana. It should be quite runny to start with, just a little thicker than the consistency of breast milk. You can dilute baby rice or purées with one of the following liquids: expressed breast milk or formula, cooled boiled tap water, or freshly squeezed vegetable or fruit juices diluted with water.

Successful weaning

To help make weaning as successful as possible:

● **Give your baby your complete attention** during the feed.

● **Begin with one regular mealtime**, whenever your baby is most hungry. This may be at the beginning or the end of the day.

● **Start off by giving a few spoons of solids** at the same time as breast-feeding.

● **Do not feel under pressure to give your baby a certain amount of food** – every baby is different. Be guided by your baby's appetite and interest in food. Babies will turn their heads away or close their mouths when they have had enough to eat.

● **Each day, offer a few more spoonfuls of food depending on your baby's appetite.** After one week, start to offer two meals a day. If feeding is going well after another one to two weeks, offer a third meal in the day.

● **Introduce new foods gradually**: not more than one every three or four days. It takes time for babies to accept new tastes, so don't despair if they spit out food. Just try again with the same purée in a couple of days' time.

● **To ensure that your baby develops a taste for savoury foods, introduce them before sweet things.** Later on, introduce mixtures of sweet and savoury; try carrot and apple or avocado and banana.

You should aim to avoid giving babies up to six months old the following foods: meat and poultry, salt, sugar, honey, citrus fruits, wheat, rye, oats, barley and their derivatives (pasta, flour, bread, cereals, except baby rice), eggs, dairy products including cheese and cow's milk, nuts, seeds, hot and spicy foods, and fish and shellfish. For more information on foods to avoid, see pages 132–3.

immune-boosting foods

During weaning it is a good idea to introduce foods that will boost the immune system. The immune system is the body's natural defence system, which will fight off infections and disease. A diet that is rich in vitamins and minerals will help to maintain a healthy immune system. Particularly important are:

A diet that is rich in vitamins and minerals will help to maintain a healthy immune system.

vitamin C

This is one of the most powerful immune-boosting nutrients, particularly useful for fighting colds. High levels are found in kiwi fruit (the richest source of this vitamin), mangoes, and broccoli.

vitamin E

Vitamin E is a powerful antioxidant. Antioxidants help to protect us against diseases such as cancer. High levels are found in avocados, sweet potatoes, and tomatoes.

Betacarotene

Betacarotene, which the body converts into vitamin A, is another good antioxidant. It is found in carrots, spinach, and peas.

zinc

Zinc is vital for a healthy immune system. It is found in rice, oats (for babies over six months), and green vegetables.

selenium

Also an antioxidant, selenium is found in avocados, fresh orange juice, and most fruits and vegetables. The selenium content of food is influenced by soil quality. Organic farms often have better quality soil, therefore choose organic.

the immune system & food allergies

Occasionally, foods that are harmless, such as nuts or milk, are perceived to be aggressive by the immune system. This is what triggers an allergic reaction. Some reactions simply cause mild discomfort, while others are life-threatening. Allergies in children seem to be on the increase, particularly asthma and eczema.

There are several ways to reduce the risk of allergies in your baby.
- **Breast-feeding helps to reduce the chance of allergies developing.**
- **Choosing organic produce** is the only way to avoid additives and chemical residues, which are now thought to cause many allergies.
- **Introduce foods individually.** If there is any sign of reaction, omit the food from the diet and try again a few weeks later. If there is a further reaction, consult your doctor or state-registered dietician or registered nutritionist. It is important not to omit something from your baby's diet without professional advice.
- **The most common allergy triggers are** cow's milk, eggs, nuts, wheat, fish, strawberries, soya products, and shellfish (see pages 132–3 for more information on foods to avoid).
- **The following foods seldom trigger allergic reactions:** rice, apples, pears, and carrots.

If, after eating something, your child's mouth or face starts to swell, he or she develops a skin rash or experiences breathing difficulties, seek medical attention immediately. Recent research indicates that peanut oil-based creams used in the treatment of eczema and other skin complaints can contribute to the development of peanut allergies, especially in children. If you are worried about your child suffering from allergies or you think food may be contributing towards problems such as eczema, seek professional advice as previously detailed.

Food intolerances are different to allergies; they don't involve the immune system and usually cause mild but constant symptoms. Most take a while to develop. The most common food intolerances are to cow's milk or wheat. They are easily prevented by excluding the food from the diet. As with suspected allergies, seek professional advice. In addition, some foods may cause hyperactivity in your child, although this affects only a tiny minority.

about the recipes

Where a dish is suitable for adults as well as babies or toddlers, I have made large quantities. Speaking from experience, it is time- and cost-efficient to make supper for all the family at the same time, even if you don't eat together. Often, all that needs adjusting for the adults is the seasoning – with herbs, spices, or just freshly ground black pepper and maybe a little salt.

These recipes are intended as a guide. Adapt the quantity of fruit, for example, to suit your own baby's tastes. For instance, if you try the Apple & Blueberry Purée on page 38 and it's not a huge hit, next time use fewer blueberries.

Similarly, suggested serving sizes are approximate. All babies and toddlers will inevitably have different appetites.

fruit purées

papaya & mango purée

makes: 2–3 servings
plus a smoothie for an adult

nutrition: vitamin C, betacarotene,
potassium, and digestive enzymes

storage: 1 day in the fridge or up to
3 months in the freezer

1 ripe papaya
1 ripe mango

Papaya and mango are great first fruits because they are naturally sweet and don't need cooking. Be sure to choose fruits that are fully ripe. If there is any left, this can be transformed into a smoothie for you by adding sparkling water or fruit juice (*see* page 79).

1 Cut the papaya in half and scoop out the seeds. Peel, then cut the flesh into cubes.
2 Slice through the mango either side of the stone. Peel, then cut the flesh into cubes.

3 Whiz the fruit with a hand-held blender or in a food processor or blender into a purée. Serve the purée as it is, or mix with a little baby rice and cooled boiled water.

banana & raspberry purée

makes: 2 servings
nutrition: vitamin C, potassium,
fibre, and energy
storage: 1 day in the fridge

1 banana, peeled
small handful of raspberries
(about 10)

Unripe bananas are indigestible for a baby's immature digestive system; it is fine to buy them slightly green but they are best eaten when the skin has a light brown speckling. Bananas are one of the most severely pesticide-treated fruits, from which their skin offers little protection. It is best to buy organic bananas, which are free of these residues. Here, banana is mixed with just a few berries so that the purée is not too acidic.

When you first introduce raspberries, you may prefer to push them through a nylon sieve before serving them to your baby in order to remove any pips.

1 Break the banana into a food processor or blender, or into a bowl if using a hand-held blender.
2 Add the raspberries and whiz until smooth. For newly weaned

babies, cook the raspberries for a minute with a little water, then add to the banana and serve when cooled.

apple & blueberry purée

makes: 2–4 servings

nutrition: vitamin C and fibre

storage: 1 day in the fridge or up to 3 months in the freezer

2 apples, peeled, cored, and cut into chunks

handful of fresh blueberries (about 30 g)

4–5 tbsp water

This is a great purée to make in the early autumn when there are lots of apples. You could always make a larger quantity and add a dollop to your breakfast cereal. Also, keep an eye open for the wild version of blueberries, bilberries. They are available in late summer and are distinctive because they have a bright blue juice.

Keep the cooking time to the absolute minimum. As soon as your baby is slightly older, start to purée raw apples without any pre-cooking. If you choose organic fruit, it is fine to include the skin in purées for older toddlers.

1 Put the apples and blueberries into a saucepan with the water.
2 Simmer for a few minutes until the apples are just tender and the blueberries have just burst open (you don't need to cook for long).

3 Whiz with a hand-held blender or in a food processor or blender until smooth. Leave to cool before serving.
4 For just-weaned babies, sieve the purée using a nylon sieve.

mango & banana purée

makes: 2–3 servings

nutrition: vitamin C, betacarotene, potassium, fibre, and energy

storage: 1 day in the fridge

½ mango

½ banana, peeled

cooled boiled water, breast milk, or formula, to thin (optional)

Mangoes are quite a strongly flavoured fruit, so when you are first introducing these fruits to your baby, you may like to add baby rice and water to make the taste slightly less intense. Bananas are rich in pectin, which aids digestion.

1 Slice through the mango either side of the stone. Peel, then cut the flesh into cubes.
2 Whiz the mango and banana with a hand-held blender or in

a food processor or blender until smooth. If you want to thin it, add a little cooled boiled water, breast milk, or formula.

melon & kiwi fruit purée

makes: 2–3 servings

nutrition: vitamins C and E, and fibre

storage: 1 day in the fridge or up to 3 months in the freezer

1 kiwi fruit, peeled and quartered

½ melon, peeled, deseeded, and roughly chopped

Kiwi fruits are a nutritional treasure – they contain twice as much vitamin C as oranges, and also aid digestion. Choose fruits that are soft to the touch, since unripe kiwi is very acidic. If you find this purée a little too thin, add some baby rice or another thickener such as banana. Or if you think it is a little too sweet, baby rice will help offset the sweetness. Leftovers make a great smoothie (*see* page 79).

Whiz the fruit with a hand-held blender or in a food processor or blender until smooth.

mango & apricot purée

makes: 2–3 servings

nutrition: vitamin C, iron, and fibre

storage: 1 day in the fridge or up to 3 months in the freezer

1 mango

2 apricots (or 1 dried apricot), peeled, stoned, and chopped

Apricots are loaded with betacarotene, believed to help reduce the risk of cancer. Choose fruits that are soft and deeply coloured. Most dried apricots are treated with sulphur dioxide, a preservative that can cause extreme allergic reactions – choose untreated, which tend to be darker in colour.

1 Cut through the mango either side of the stone. Peel, then cut the flesh into cubes.
2 Whiz the mango and apricots with a hand-held blender or in a food processor or blender to a smooth purée.

veg purées

pea & potato purée

makes: 2–3 servings

nutrition: B vitamins and vitamin C, fibre, and folic acid

storage: 1 day in the fridge or up to 3 months in the freezer

2–3 potatoes, peeled and chopped

60 g (or 2 large handfuls) shelled peas

mint leaves (optional)

The nutritional quality and flavour of vegetables – potatoes in particular – is very much dependent on soil quality. You may wish to buy organic potatoes since so many chemicals can be stored in their skins. Use fresh peas when in season, and remember that they don't take long to cook. Your baby should enjoy the fresh sweet taste of peas mixed with the starchy potato.

1 Bring a small pan of water to the boil, add the potatoes, and cook until tender. Alternatively, steam until tender.

2 A couple of minutes before they are cooked, add the peas and cook until just tender.

3 Drain, add the mint, if using, and whiz with a hand-held blender or in a food processor or blender until smooth. Leave to cool before serving.

avocado & broad bean purée

makes: 2–3 servings

nutrition: essential fatty acids, potassium, and vitamins A and E

storage: eat immediately

60 g broad beans, fresh if possible, skinned (gently squeeze each pod and the green centre will come out)

1 avocado, peeled, stoned, and chopped

Avocados that are rock hard may have been kept in cold storage for too long and will often go black inside instead of ripening. Choose avocados that are ripe and that give to gentle pressure. It may seem like a real drag skinning broad beans, but it makes for a very smooth purée, which is easier for your baby to digest. This is also delicious on toast for adults.

1 Bring a pan of water to the boil, add the beans, and cook for one minute. Drain and leave to cool.

2 Whiz the avocado and beans with a hand-held blender or in a food processor or blender until smooth.

Italian-style vegetable purée

makes: 5 servings plus
1 adult serving

nutrition: vitamins C and E, and fibre

storage: 48 hours in the fridge or up
to 3 months in the freezer

1 tbsp light and fruity olive oil

1 shallot, finely chopped

1 aubergine, finely chopped

2 red peppers, cored, deseeded, and
finely chopped

2 courgettes, finely chopped

4 plum tomatoes, chopped

a few basil leaves

This is a great recipe for using any vegetables that you have to hand. For babies that are just starting the weaning process, try a combination of tomatoes, courgettes, and a little baby rice, since the flavours here may be too intense. Try this combination once they have been eating solids for at least a month. Any leftovers will always make a great pasta sauce.

1 Heat the oil in a frying pan, add the shallot, and sauté until soft.

2 Add the aubergine, peppers, and courgettes, and cook for five minutes.

3 Add the tomatoes and continue to cook for another eight minutes. Add the basil. Remove a serving for yourself and enjoy with pasta and grated cheese on top.

4 Purée the rest for the baby with a hand-held blender or in a food processor or blender.

garden vegetable purée

makes: 3–4 servings

nutrition: vitamins A, C, and E, and folic acid

storage: 24 hours in the fridge or up to 3 months in the freezer

1 potato or sweet potato, peeled and chopped

¼ swede, peeled and chopped

½ parsnip, peeled and chopped

1 carrot, peeled and chopped

To ensure that these root vegetables cook evenly, try to chop them into even chunks. If you have any leftovers, add enough stock to make a bowl of soup for your lunch.

1 Put the potato, swede, parsnip, and carrot into a colander and rest over a pan of simmering water. Cover with a lid and steam for 10 minutes until tender.

2 Allow to cool slightly before whizzing with a hand-held blender or in a food processor or blender until smooth.

3 Leave to cool a little more before serving.

sweet potato, leek, & pea purée

makes: 3 servings

nutrition: vitamins A, C, and E, and folic acid

storage: 24 hours in the fridge or up to 3 months in the freezer

1 sweet potato, peeled and chopped
¼ leek, sliced
60 g shelled peas

Like ordinary potatoes, sweet potatoes retain chemical residues in their skins, so you may wish to choose organic. You could double the quantities and make this into a soup for yourself – just thin it with some vegetable stock.

1 Put the sweet potato into a colander and rest over a pan of simmering water. Cover with a lid and steam for six minutes.
2 Add the leek and peas to the sweet potato and continue steaming for another four minutes.
3 Allow to cool slightly before whizzing with a hand-held blender or in a food processor or blender until smooth. Serve warm.

roast pepper & potato purée

makes: 3 servings

nutrition: B vitamins and vitamin C, betacarotene, folic acid, and fibre

storage: 24 hours in the fridge or up to 3 months in the freezer

½ red pepper, cored, deseeded, and quartered
2 medium potatoes, peeled and chopped

Babies will enjoy the sweetness and colour of red pepper.

1 Preheat the grill to a high heat.
2 Grill the pepper quarters skin side up for five to 10 minutes until black and blistered all over. While still hot, transfer to a plastic bag and tie tightly.
3 Put the potatoes into a colander and rest over a pan of simmering water. Cover with a lid and steam for 10 minutes until tender.
4 When the pepper has cooled, remove all the blackened skin.
5 Allow the potatoes to cool slightly before whizzing them with the pepper with a hand-held blender or in a food processor or blender until smooth. Serve warm.

As your baby becomes more used to solids, it is important to introduce a nutritionally rich range of foods.

At this stage, milk is still your baby's primary food. However, solid food is becoming more important as a nutritional source. Many babies will start to teethe around this time, which helps them cope with lumpier food, although the development of primary teeth (milk teeth) can vary. Some babies are born with a tooth and others have no teeth until they are a year old.

For the first few weeks, weaning is a learning experience for both you and your baby – more about texture and new sensations than specific nutrients. As your baby becomes more used to solids, it is important to introduce a nutritionally rich range of foods. It is also important to give your baby water.

The foods

You should aim to include the following in your baby's developing diet:

● **Fish, lean meat, and poultry** (except smoked fish and smoked meats). Aim to offer one of these at least once a week. These are excellent sources of iron, which is

weaning
6–8 months

very important at this stage. Babies are born with a natural store of iron, which becomes depleted at around six months. Unless it is replenished, growth and development can be adversely affected. For more information on iron, *see* page 11.

- **Red and brown lentils, chick-peas, black-eyed peas, and haricot, flageolet, and kidney beans** – make sure they are very well cooked and puréed so that they are easy for the baby to digest. These are all rich in carbohydrates, fibre, B vitamins, folic acid, selenium, iron, and zinc.
- **Wheat or wheat-based foods**, e.g. pasta, cereals, and wholemeal bread. These foods are a great way to encourage babies to chew and use their jaw muscles.
- **Cow's milk only as part of a dish**, e.g. Broccoli & Cauliflower Cheese, page 69, and Coconut Rice Pudding with Tropical Fruit, page 48. If you prefer, try goat's or sheep's milk, or soya drinks fortified with calcium.

- **Small amounts of dairy products**, particularly live yogurt.
- **Water.** Encourage your baby to drink water in between meals and milk-feeds – cooled, boiled tap water is best.
- **Nuts and nut butters.** These can be given as long as they are finely ground to prevent your baby from choking. If there is any history of allergy in your family, avoid peanuts and foods containing peanuts. *See* pages 132–3 for more information.
- **Citrus fruits.** These can be gradually introduced, although it is best to mix them with other foods, e.g. banana, oats, or rice.
- **Dried fruits.** They should be introduced a little at a time, and always puréed; if you serve too many at one time, they may come back out faster than they went in!

successful weaning

Aim for three small meals a day. Introduce foods with more texture and shape, e.g. tiny pasta shapes. Make the purées slightly lumpy.

If he shows an interest, let your baby feed himself, with either a spoon or fingers. Try offering foods that can be easily held, e.g. bread, slices of peeled soft fruit, or cooked vegetables. Finger foods encourage chewing, which can help with teething pains, the development of speech muscles, and self-feeding.

You should aim to avoid giving babies up to eight months old the following foods: cow's milk as a drink, eggs, salt, excessive sugar, and honey. For more information about foods to avoid, *see* pages 132–3.

fruit dishes

mashed banana, cinnamon, & yogurt

makes: 1–2 servings

nutrition: vitamins A, B, and C, folic acid, potassium, and magnesium

storage: 1 day in the fridge

1 banana, peeled and mashed

2 tbsps natural or soya yogurt

pinch of ground cinnamon

Bananas are a high-energy food and are easily digested. Dairy products such as yogurt can have high amounts of chemical residues and antibiotics, commonly used in dairy herds so you may wish to choose organic. Also, try to use "live" yogurt, which is full of good bacteria that helps with digestion.

Whiz all the ingredients together with a hand-held blender or in a food processor or blender until smooth. Serve.

apricot porridge

makes: 4–6 servings

nutrition: protein, calcium, potassium, vitamin B, fibre, and energy

storage: 24 hours in the fridge or up to 3 months in the freezer

125 ml boiling water

10 ready-to-eat dried apricots, finely chopped

60 g oats

125 ml milk or soya drink

Oats have a good nutritional content, providing minerals and vitamins essential for strong bones and healthy teeth. Choose raw natural oats, ideally cold-rolled. Also choose dried apricots not treated with sulphur dioxide. This dish is also a delicious breakfast dish for an adult.

1 Pour the boiling water over the apricots and leave to soak for half an hour.
2 Put all the ingredients into a saucepan, cover, and heat gently for five minutes, stirring often, until the mixture has thickened.
3 Purée with a hand-held blender or in a food processor or blender, adding a little more milk or soya drink to thin if necessary.

apple & pear porridge

makes: 4–6 servings

nutrition: protein, calcium, potassium, vitamin B, fibre, and energy

storage: 24 hours in the fridge or up to 3 months in the freezer

60 g oats

125 ml milk or soya drink

125 ml boiling water

1 ripe apple and 1 ripe pear, peeled, cored, and chopped into small chunks

2 tbsps sultanas

This porridge is ideal in the autumn, when there are lots of apples and pears around. It makes a good breakfast dish for adults too, particularly if you add a pinch of cinnamon. Babies may enjoy a little of this spice once they have been taking solids for at least a month.

1 Put all the ingredients into a saucepan and heat gently for five minutes, stirring often, until the mixture has thickened.

2 Purée with a hand-held blender or in a food processor or blender, adding a little more milk, soya drink, or cooled boiled water to thin if necessary.

oats with apple

makes: 4–6 servings

nutrition: protein, calcium, potassium, vitamin B, fibre, and energy

storage: 24 hours in the fridge

60 g porridge oats or oatmeal

125 ml milk or soya drink

1 apple, finely grated

This is a very refreshing and filling breakfast to start the day, which children and adults alike will love. It is also good with yogurt and honey for older babies. If you use organic apples, it's fine to leave the skin on as long as it's washed and finely grated.

1 Soak the oats or oatmeal in milk or soya drink overnight in the fridge.

2 The next day, stir in the grated apple.

3 Add a little extra milk, soya drink, or cooled boiled water to thin the mixture, if required, just before serving.

coconut rice pudding with tropical fruit

makes: 2–3 servings plus
1–2 adult servings

nutrition: energy, calcium,
magnesium, and vitamin C

storage: 24 hours, but serve cold
(never reheat rice – it is one of
the commonest causes
of food poisoning)

150 g short-grain pudding rice

250 ml milk or soya drink

250 ml coconut milk (do not serve
nuts or their products to babies if
there is any family history of allergies)

100 ml water

½ tsp vanilla extract

1–2 tsps golden caster sugar (or
preferably omit altogether)

1 small knob unsalted butter

1 ripe papaya

1 ripe mango

This dish is ideal for grown-ups as well as babies – just squeeze some lime juice over the fruit before serving.

1 Put the first five ingredients into a saucepan and stir.
2 Bring to the boil, then reduce the heat and simmer for 15 to 20 minutes, stirring often to prevent the mixture from sticking on the bottom. If necessary, add a few more tablespoons of water to thin the mixture.
3 Add the sugar, if using, and butter; mix well, and cook for another minute. Deseed the papaya, then peel and dice the flesh.
4 Cut through the mango either side of the stone. Peel, then cut the flesh into cubes. Serve the fruit with the rice pudding.

veg dishes

sweet potato & ginger purée with lamb

makes: 3–4 servings
plus 1 adult serving

nutrition: vitamins C and E,
and protein

storage: 24 hours in the fridge or
up to 3 months in the freezer

300 g sweet potatoes, peeled and
cut into large chunks

1 small knob of butter

1 tsp grated ginger

pinch of grated nutmeg

freshly ground black pepper (optional)

1 lamb chop (or cook 2 if you are
eating the sweet potato
purée as well)

A good tip for grating ginger is to keep it in the freezer. It then grates very finely without being fibrous, making it easier for little ones to eat. This is also delicious for adults – serve with grilled chicken breasts instead of lamb chops if you prefer. To warm through, cover with foil and pop into a moderate oven for 20 minutes.

1 Preheat the grill to a medium heat.

2 Put the sweet-potato chunks in a saucepan, cover with water, and cook for 15 to 20 minutes until soft. Drain and return to the pan.

3 Add the butter, ginger, and nutmeg, and mash together well. Season with a little pepper, if desired.

4 Meanwhile, grill the lamb chop(s) for a few minutes each side (depending on thickness) until cooked through.

5 Finely chop the lamb into tiny pieces and mix into the potato purée. Alternatively, for a smoother purée, whiz the potato and lamb with a hand-held blender or in a food processor or blender.

lentil & butternut soup

makes: 2 servings plus
1–2 adult servings

nutrition: protein, betacarotene,
calcium, and potassium

storage: 48 hours in the fridge or up
to 3 months in the freezer

1 tbsp olive oil

1 onion, finely chopped

½ fennel bulb, trimmed
and finely chopped

1 butternut squash (about 1.5 kg),
peeled, deseeded, and diced

180 g red lentils

700 ml boiling water or very weak
vegetable stock

2 handfuls baby pasta,
e.g. stars or hoops

1 handful parsley,
finely chopped (optional)

juice of ½ lemon

pieces of soft bread, for chewing

As your child gets older, start to be a little more adventurous and serve soups made with lentils or other pulses. In order to make it easier for the baby to consume, add some baby pasta to thicken. Purée before or after you have added the pasta, depending on your preference for your baby. Once you have given your baby his meal, sit down and enjoy a bowl yourself.

1 Heat the oil in a saucepan, add the onion, and sweat until soft.
2 Add the fennel and squash, and cook for a few minutes.
3 Add the lentils and boiling water or stock and simmer for 15 minutes, or until both lentils and squash are tender. Transfer to a bowl, and using a hand-held blender, purée until you have a smooth, even consistency, or purée in a food processor or blender. Return to the pan, add the pasta, and cook according to the packet instructions.
4 Add the parsley, if using, and lemon juice. Serve with pieces of soft bread.

vegetable gratin

makes: 3–4 servings plus 1 adult serving

nutrition: protein, vitamin C, calcium, and zinc

storage: 24 hours in the fridge or up to 3 months in the freezer

60 g cauliflower

60 g broccoli

1 carrot

½ leek

150 ml milk or soya drink

10 g plain flour

10 g unsalted butter

50 g Cheddar cheese

handful of flat-leaf parsley, finely chopped (optional)

This dish makes a great light supper for adults – just add some seasoning when you serve it to grown-ups.

1 Cut all the vegetables into bite-sized pieces, then put into a steamer or into a colander and rest over a pan of simmering water.

2 Cover and steam for four to six minutes until tender.

3 To make a quick white sauce, mix together the milk or soya drink, flour, and butter in a saucepan. Heat gently, stirring constantly, until you have a smooth sauce. Bring to the boil and remove from the heat. Leave to cool slightly, then stir in the cheese.

4 Place the vegetables in a bowl and pour the sauce over. Sprinkle with parsley, if using.

fish

plaice with a tomato, courgette, & bean sauce

makes: 4–5 servings or 2–3 servings plus 1 adult serving

nutrition: protein, B vitamins and vitamin C, iron, zinc, and iodine

storage: 24 hours in the fridge or up to 3 months in the freezer

1 tbsp olive oil

1 onion, finely chopped

3 beef tomatoes, roughly chopped

100 ml water

1 courgette, finely chopped

60 g thin green beans, finely chopped

4 plaice fillets, skinned

This makes a handy lunch or supper dish for all the family and is particularly good with baked potatoes or pasta.

1 Heat the oil in a flameproof casserole dish or saucepan, add the onion, and sweat over medium-low heat for five minutes until soft.

2 Add the tomatoes and cook for about two minutes. Stir in the water, then transfer to a bowl and purée with a hand-held blender, or in a food processor or blender.

3 Return to the pan. Add the courgette and beans, and cook for five minutes.

4 Check the plaice fillets for any stray bones, then carefully roll up from the tail end and place in the sauce.

5 Spoon over some of the sauce to prevent the fish drying out. Cover the pan and simmer for five minutes.

Babies have developed in many ways by the time they reach eight months of age. They will be able to sit on their own and will be more aware of things around them. They are likely to be able to pick up and put down spoons or cups and pass food from hand to mouth. They may be interested in drinking from a cup – with your help! With new teeth, they can now cope with finely chopped food rather than purées.

The next few months are equally exciting as the first eight months, since your baby will show signs of crawling, which will soon progress to standing and, eventually, walking. By one year, most babies will probably respond to their names and will start to say a few simple words like "mama" and "dada". As they become more active and energy levels grow, they will need more food and a more varied diet of three to four feeds a day. You should encourage a daily routine for sleeping and eating. It is also vital to make sure that your baby or toddler drinks plenty of liquids.

8-12 months

Your baby is now much more alert and inquisitive, and should be ready for new tastes and textures. There are lots of new foods you can introduce and many ways of preparing them that make them more appealing to your baby.

Meals should be as interesting as possible. Offer varied textures – ingredients can be grated, mashed, or finely chopped instead of puréed. Use foods that have more intense flavours such as red fruit or herbs, which can be added to savoury dishes. Soft finger foods such as cucumber, mango, cheese, and bread may be offered. At first, your baby may suck finger foods, but eventually he or she will be able to chew them. Once a baby is more confident, try slightly harder foods such as toast and peeled apples.

guidelines for a healthy diet

Follow the guidelines below to help make feeding as successful as possible at this stage.

● **Slowly reduce the frequency and quantity of milk-feeds:** aim for about 500 to 600 ml a day. Try to give milk after meals only – it will take the edge off your baby's appetite if given before solid food.
● **Aim for three meals a day,** fitting in with the family routine, offering healthy snacks and drinks in between.
● **It is important to give babies lots of water;** fluid is needed to help their bodies work properly and prevent constipation. The best drinks to offer are cooled, boiled water or diluted fruit juice. It is advised that fruit juice is offered diluted until the baby is at least nine months old.
● **Keep on introducing new foods,** even if there is resistance at first. Babies learn to like most things eventually. However, be aware that at this stage, babies will close their mouths firmly or turn their heads away when they are full.
● **Establish meals as happy occasions.** Talk to your baby when feeding and give him or her lots of encouragement. Avoid distractions such as television during meals.

ingredients

When you are planning meals, consider including the following new ingredients:
● **Eggs** are a great source of protein, but must be well-cooked.
● **Increase the amount of dairy foods,** especially cheese and live yogurt. Offer the full-fat variety, because babies need fat to supply them with energy for growth.
● **Diluted fruit juice.** Offer at meal-times, not to sip at all day, since this will encourage tooth decay.
● **Offer full fat cow's milk** only as part of a dish, rather than as a drink.

Avoid giving babies up to 10 months old: cow's milk as a drink, soft eggs, soft cheese, salt, excessive sugar, honey, coffee, or tea. If there is any history of allergy in your family, avoid peanuts and foods containing them. For more

8–10 months

Keep on introducing new foods, even if there is resistance at first. Babies learn to like most things eventually.

red rice with fish (see photo on page 57)

makes: 3–4 servings plus 1–2 adult servings

nutrition: protein, potassium, and vitamin C

storage: rice should not be reheated but can be served cold up to 24 hours

1 tbsp olive oil

1 shallot, finely chopped

1 clove garlic, crushed

150 g red rice

1 tsp tomato purée or sun-dried tomato purée

600 ml weak no-salt vegetable stock

½ yellow pepper, cored, deseeded, and finely chopped

50 g green beans, finely sliced

125 g cherry tomatoes, quartered

2–3 chestnut mushrooms, quartered

freshly ground black pepper

450 g cod fillets

200 ml milk

1 bay leaf

4 black peppercorns

1 tbsp finely chopped flat-leaf parsley

Organic red rice, from the Camargue in France, has a nutty texture and wonderful colour. Rice and fish are both good sources of protein and the vegetables provide vitamins and minerals.

Use this recipe as a guide and add any vegetables that you have to hand. You could also add little pieces of poached chicken to the rice instead of fish. This is another example of a dish that can be served to both toddlers and adults, so I have deliberately made more than you will need for just your baby. If you want less, simply halve the ingredients.

1 Heat the oil in a saucepan, add the shallot and garlic, and cook gently for a minute or two.
2 Add the rice, tomato purée, and stock. Cover and simmer for 25 minutes. Add the yellow pepper, beans, tomatoes, and mushrooms and cook for another five minutes. Drain any excess stock and season with pepper.

3 While the rice is cooking, put the fish, skin-side up, in a saucepan, pour on the milk, add the bay leaf and peppercorns, and cover. Cook over a low heat for five to six minutes
4 Strain the fish, removing the skin, and flake the flesh, carefully checking for and removing any stray bones. Mix the parsley into the rice and serve with the fish scattered over the top.

basic couscous

makes: 2–3 servings
nutrition: calcium and potassium
storage: 24 hours in the fridge

200 g couscous
250 ml boiling vegetable stock

Couscous is really quick and easy to cook, and makes a great alternative to pasta or potatoes. Good things to add to couscous: finely chopped tomatoes, chopped herbs, chopped cooked vegetables, melted butter, and grated cheese.

1 Put the couscous into a heat-proof bowl. Pour on the stock, stir, then cover with a plate. Leave for 15 minutes.

2 Fluff up with a fork. Serve warm or cold. It is delicious with stew.

fruity couscous with chicken

makes: 2–3 servings
nutrition: protein, vitamin B$_{12}$, and zinc
storage: 24 hours in the fridge

200 g couscous
100 ml freshly squeezed orange juice
150 ml boiling water
2–3 boneless, skinless chicken breasts
1 tbsp olive oil
8–10 ready-to-eat dried apricots, puréed
a few coriander leaves
2–3 tbsps natural yogurt
freshly ground black pepper

Children love the combination of sweet fruit with chicken. Try to avoid waxed oranges – it is only done to make them shiny!

1 Put the couscous into a heat-proof bowl. Mix the orange juice with the boiling water and pour over the couscous, quickly stir, then cover with a plate. Leave for 15 minutes.
2 Cut the chicken breasts into thin strips. Heat the oil in a frying pan and fry the chicken for a few minutes on each side until golden and cooked through.

3 Chop the chicken into tiny pieces, then stir into the couscous with the apricots, coriander, and yogurt. Season with pepper to taste and serve.

mushroom ragu with herby mash

makes: 2 servings plus 1–2 adult servings

nutrition: protein, fibre, potassium, and vitamins B_{12} and C

storage: 48 hours in the fridge or up to 3 months in the freezer

20 g dried porcini mushrooms

1 tbsp olive oil

1 onion, finely chopped

1 clove garlic, crushed

300 g mushrooms, cut into bite-sized pieces

2 tsps tomato purée

250 ml tomato passata (sieved puréed tomatoes, available in supermarkets) or canned chopped tomatoes

1 tbsp mixed chopped herbs, e.g. oregano, basil, and thyme

freshly ground black pepper

for the mash

700 g potatoes, peeled and cut into quarters

100 ml milk

20 g butter

1 tbsp finely chopped parsley

Potatoes are highly nutritious. They are also a brilliant weaning food, because the starches in them are easily digestible. For this dish you can use any mushrooms you like – try brown cap or field mushrooms and, since they have a really rich flavour, cut them as small as you like.

1 Put the porcini mushrooms into a heat-proof bowl, cover with boiling water, and leave to soak for 15 minutes.

2 Lift out and squeeze any liquid from the mushrooms, then finely chop. Strain the liquid through a piece of kitchen paper to remove any grit and reserve the liquid.

3 Heat the olive oil in a large saucepan and sweat the onion slowly, without colouring, for five to 10 minutes. Add the garlic and cook for a further two minutes. Add all the mushrooms and one tablespoon of the porcini soaking liquid. Stir once, then cover and cook for five minutes over a low heat. Once the mushrooms have softened, add the tomato purée and the remaining porcini soaking liquid. Turn the heat down and leave to cook for 10 minutes.

4 Add the passata or chopped tomatoes, herbs, and pepper to taste, and cook for a further 10 minutes.

5 While the ragu is cooking, boil the potatoes until just tender. Drain well, then add the milk and butter and mash until smooth and creamy. Stir in the parsley. Serve with the mushroom ragu.

cheesy macaroni with bolognese sauce & aubergine

makes: 2–3 servings plus 1–2 adult servings

nutrition: iron, protein, vitamin C, and carbohydrates

storage: the Bolognese sauce can be kept in the fridge for 48 hours or in the freezer for up to 3 months

1 tbsp olive oil

1 onion, finely chopped

1 clove garlic, crushed

500 g lamb mince

½ aubergine, chopped into small cubes

1 carrot, chopped into small cubes

1 celery stick, chopped into small cubes

400 g vine tomatoes, chopped, or 400 g canned chopped tomatoes

3 tbsps chopped mixed herbs, e.g. oregano, basil, parsley, and thyme

150 g macaroni

10 g Parmesan cheese, grated

10 g Cheddar cheese, grated

A quick Bolognese sauce made with lamb is an ideal way to introduce a little meat into your baby's diet. Pasta is another great staple food for children and infant and toddler pasta shapes are available, too.

1 Heat the olive oil in a saucepan and sweat the onion slowly, without colouring, for five to eight minutes.
2 Add the garlic and cook for a further two minutes.
3 Add the lamb mince and brown, stirring often to break up the meat.
4 Add the aubergine, carrot, and celery, and cook for five minutes.
5 Add the tomatoes and herbs, cover, and cook for a further 10 to 15 minutes.

6 Meanwhile, bring a large pan of water to the boil and cook the macaroni according to the packet instructions. To serve, sprinkle the grated cheeses over the macaroni and spoon the Bolognese sauce on top.

scrambled eggs

makes: 1–2 servings
nutrition: protein, vitamins A , B$_{12}$, and E, and zinc
storage: best eaten fresh

2 eggs
freshly ground black pepper
knob of unsalted butter

Scrambled eggs is one of the quickest and most versatile meals for all the family – and makes an ideal baby breakfast, lunch or supper. Try adding chopped herbs (especially chives) or mushrooms – the list is endless. You may wish to feed your baby organic eggs as they are free from antibiotics and artificial colourants commonly used in intensive egg production.

1 In a bowl, beat the eggs well and add a little pepper.
2 Put the butter in a pan. When it is foaming, add the eggs and stir frequently with a wooden spoon to stop the egg sticking.

3 Take the pan off the heat while it is very slightly liquid, so that the eggs are not overcooked. Serve with fingers of bread or toast.

scrambled egg with spring onion, tomatoes, & ham

makes: 1–2 servings
nutrition: protein, vitamins A, B$_{12}$, and E, and zinc
storage: best eaten fresh

small knob of unsalted butter
1 spring onion, finely chopped
2 eggs
freshly ground black pepper
1 slice of ham, chopped
1 tomato, chopped

This is a great dish for babies because it has lots of colours and textures, which are important for encouraging your baby to chew.

1 Melt the butter in a pan and cook the spring onion for one to two minutes until soft.
2 In a bowl, beat the eggs well and add a little pepper. Stir in the ham and tomato. Pour into the pan with the onion and stir frequently with a wooden spoon to stop the egg sticking.

3 Take the pan off the heat while it is very slightly liquid, so that the eggs are not overcooked. Serve with fingers of bread or toast.

berry ripple fool

makes: 3–4 servings

nutrition: calcium, vitamin B_2, and zinc

storage: 24 hours in the fridge

125 g blueberries

125 g blackberries

200 ml natural yogurt

for the custard

200 ml milk

1 vanilla pod, split open lengthways

3 egg yolks

1 tsp caster sugar

1 tbsp cornflour

If you are able to get to a farmers' market, look out for bilberries, the British-grown version of the blueberry, which are usually available in late summer. They have a darker, sweeter juice and an altogether more intense flavour. If you can't find fresh, use frozen berries.

1 To make the custard, heat the milk with the vanilla pod in a saucepan until just below boiling point.

2 In a bowl, mix the egg yolks, sugar, and cornflour together, then pour over the hot milk, stirring constantly. Return to the saucepan and heat, stirring constantly, until the mixture thickens. Do not allow to boil, otherwise it will curdle.

Once the custard has thickened, leave it to cool.

3 Meanwhile, purée the berries together with a hand-held blender or in a food processor or blender. Gently fold together the cooled custard and yogurt. Swirl through the fruit purée to make a rippled fool.

fruity muesli

makes: about 750 g (lots of breakfasts!)

nutrition: fibre, potassium, and iron

storage: up to 2 weeks in an airtight container

40 g sunflower seeds

125 g almonds or hazelnuts, toasted (do not give nuts to babies if there is any family history of allergies)

50 g unsweetened desiccated coconut

4 tbsps wheat germ

330 g rolled oats

pinch of ground cinnamon

125 g ready-to-eat dried apricots or other dried fruit, puréed

75 g dried dates, puréed

Balanced and energy-packed, muesli makes a great breakfast for children and adults alike. You must grind the muesli before serving to prevent your baby from choking. You could just whiz half the dry mixture and keep some aside for yourself. Vary this basic recipe by adding different dried fruit, such as apple or pineapple.

1 Dry-fry the seeds and nuts in a frying pan, stirring constantly, until golden brown. This will take about five minutes. Leave to cool.

2 Put the seeds, nuts, coconut, and wheat germ into a food processor and whiz to a fine powder.

3 Tip into a bowl and mix through the oats, cinnamon, and dried fruit. Serve with milk or formula.

stewed apple & rhubarb with custard

makes: 4–5 servings

nutrition: calcium, potassium, and vitamins A and C

storage: 4 days in the fridge or the stewed fruit can be kept in the freezer for up to 3 months

6 Cox's apples, peeled, cored, and chopped

1 large stick of rhubarb, chopped

50 ml apple juice

custard (*see* page 64) or thick natural yogurt, to serve

Avoid "forced" rhubarb, which has a lower nutrient content. Choose rhubarb that is firm and pink. Rhubarb can be quite sour because of its high acid content. Here, I have used apple juice to sweeten it instead of sugar. This also makes a great base for a crumble.

1 Put the apples, rhubarb, and apple juice into a saucepan.
2 Cover and cook over a low to medium-low heat for 10 to 15 minutes until the fruit is tender.
3 Serve with custard or thick natural yogurt.

red fruit compote

makes: 2–3 servings

nutrition: vitamins C and E, and potassium

storage: 2–3 days in the fridge or up to 2 months in the freezer

1 apple, peeled, cored, and thinly sliced

100 g red berries, e.g. raspberries, blackcurrants, blackberries, or blueberries

100 g strawberries

This dish has quite an intense flavour, so you may wish to thin it with a little water or juice. It is delicious with some yogurt swirled through. This is great to make in the summer when lots of soft fruit is readily available. Always use a nylon sieve for sieving the fruit, since metal may react with the acid in the fruit and give the finished dish an unpleasant taste.

1 Put the apple and all the berries, except the strawberries, into a saucepan with one tablespoon of water.
2 Cook over a gentle heat for two to three minutes until the fruit starts to release juice and the apple is soft. Remove from the heat and leave to cool. Push through a nylon sieve into a bowl.
3 Wash and hull the strawberries. Dice, then mix into the fruit purée.

vanilla risotto

makes: 2 servings plus 1–2 adult servings

nutrition: protein, calcium, and vitamin B$_2$

storage: 24 hours in the fridge (do not reheat)

25 g unsalted butter

175 g arborio rice

600 ml milk

1 vanilla pod, split open lengthways, or 3 tsps vanilla extract

This goes really well with either soft, fresh or stewed fruit.

1 Preheat the oven to 180°C/350°F/gas mark 4.
2 Melt the butter in a heavy-based pan and add the rice. Stir, thoroughly coating with the butter, for a minute or two until you hear the rice make a hissing sound, which means it is now ready to add the liquid.
3 Add a quarter of the milk and the vanilla pod or extract. Stir well and bring up to simmering point.

Add the remaining milk and bring up to simmering point again. Stir once, then transfer to a warm ovenproof dish.
4 Place in the oven on the middle shelf without covering.
5 After 15 minutes, remove from the oven and give it a good stir. Return to the oven for 10 minutes. Remove from the oven and stir again. Leave to stand for one to two minutes before serving.

almond milk

makes: 2 servings

nutrition: vitamin E, minerals, and protein, especially for vegetarians

storage: 24 hours in the fridge

100 g blanched whole or flaked almonds (do not give nuts to babies if there is any family history of allergies)

250 ml cold water

This is an ultra-quick and easy drink, and an excellent source of protein for vegetarians. It also makes a great substitute for milk or yogurt in smoothies. Buy nuts from shops with a rapid turnover and store them in the fridge, since old nuts go rancid and will taste terrible.

1 Put the almonds into a food processor or blender with the water.
2 Whiz together at a high speed for two to three minutes until a thick, white milk has formed. For small babies or for a smoother texture, pour through a sieve. If you are going to use the milk in a shake or smoothie, there is no need to strain it. If there are a lot of chunky bits, you haven't blended it for long enough.

Feeding gradually becomes more and more exciting for your baby as he or she approaches toddlerhood. Babies should have an established eating routine. Aim for three meals a day with a couple of healthy snacks between meals – celery sticks spread with peanut butter (unless allergic to nuts, *see* page 132), chunks of Cheddar, carrot or cucumber sticks, rusks, crackers, and dried fruit.

successful feeding

Children establish eating habits at an early age, so it's important to show them that food can be healthy and fun. Encourage your child to eat new things, but try to avoid confrontations over food. You can disguise less popular foods with a bit of inventiveness; try adding brightly coloured vegetables such as sweetcorn or *petit pois* to mashed carrot or broccoli.

Children often love eating things that are easy for them to hold: try baby tomatoes, baby corn, or mange-tout.

planning meals

You still need to be feeding your baby 500 to 600 ml of breast milk or formula a day. As your baby becomes more active, he or she will need a good start to the day. Encourage babies at breakfast time with lots of variations. Make quick baby-friendly cereal by whizzing organic sugar-free muesli or other organic cereals in a food processor.

Just after breakfast is a good time to offer babies some breast milk or formula; they will be more willing for a larger meal after a good night's sleep.

Your baby should have a healthy diet, but that doesn't mean excluding fat – babies need the calories for energy and to absorb fat-soluble vitamins. Good sources of fat are yogurt, cheese, olive oil, avocados, nuts, and seeds.

Babies under a year old need some fibre, but it should be soluble fibre which is found in peas, fruit, and vegetable juices (*see* page 9).

This is a good time to introduce your baby to a wider range of naturally dried fruit. They are a great source of vitamins, minerals, and soluble fibre. Try to stick to dried fruit that hasn't been treated with colour-preserving sulphur dioxide. Dried fruit should be given in moderation because it is high in fruit sugar.

Introduce foods with more intense flavours. Try herbs such as parsley and basil, onions, garlic, leeks, and mild spices such as cinnamon and ginger. All of these are available organically and will have a more pronounced flavour, as well as being higher in nutrients and free of chemical residues.

Avoid giving babies up to 12 months old the following foods: cow's milk as a drink, salt, excessive sugar, honey, coffee, or tea. If there is any history of allergy in your family, avoid nuts and foods containing nuts. For more information about foods to avoid, *see* pages 132–3.

10–12 months

Children establish eating habits at an early age, so it's important to show them that food can be healthy and fun.

herby chicken with potato purée

makes: 4–6 servings or 2–4 servings plus 2 adult servings

nutrition: protein, minerals, and B vitamins

storage: 24 hours in the fridge and then served cold (best not reheated)

4 boneless, skinless chicken breasts

180 ml Greek yogurt

1 tbsp olive oil

1 clove garlic, crushed

2 tbsps chopped herbs, e.g. parsley, coriander, or thyme

lemon wedges (optional) and steamed green vegetables, to serve

for the potato purée

700 g potatoes

50 ml olive oil and 50 ml milk

The yogurt marinade helps to tenderize the chicken, making it very moist and therefore easy to chew for those with only a few teeth. The subtle, herby flavour is usually a favourite with little ones.

1 Put the chicken breasts flat into a plastic bag and bash with a rolling pin until they are an even thickness.

2 Mix together the yogurt, olive oil, garlic, herbs, and freshly ground black pepper to taste. Spoon the yogurt marinade over the chicken breasts, cover, and refrigerate for a couple of hours.

3 Cook the potatoes in boiling water until just tender, drain, and return to a low heat for a minute to cook off any remaining water. Mash with the olive oil and milk.

4 Preheat a grill to a high heat. Transfer the chicken to a baking tray and grill for five minutes on each side, basting with the marinade as it cooks.

5 If using, squeeze some juice from the lemon wedges over the chicken before slicing the chicken into thin strips. Serve with the creamy mash and green vegetables such as spinach, beans, or broccoli.

broccoli & cauliflower cheese

makes: 2 servings

nutrition: vitamins A and C, and calcium

storage: 48 hours in the fridge or up to 3 months in the freezer

4 small broccoli florets

4 small cauliflower florets

10 g unsalted butter

10 g plain flour

about 150 ml liquid – a mixture of vegetable water and either formula, milk, or soya drink

10 g mild Cheddar cheese, finely grated

A little cheese sauce mixed with vegetables is a good way to incorporate the dairy foods milk, cheese, and butter into your baby's diet. Most members of the cabbage family, such as cauliflower and broccoli, are highly nutritious.

1 Bring a small amount of water to the boil, add the vegetables, and cook until just tender. Drain and cut into small pieces.

2 Melt the butter in a saucepan, add the flour, and cook for a few minutes. Gradually add enough of the liquid to make a sauce with a thin, smooth consistency. Leave to cool slightly, then add the cheese and stir until melted.

3 Pour the sauce over the vegetables and serve. Alternatively, whiz the vegetables and sauce with a hand-held blender or in a food processor or blender until smooth.

cod & salmon cakes with fruity salsa

makes: 10–15 little fish cakes

nutrition: protein and carbohydrate

storage: 24 hours in the fridge or up to 3 months in the freezer

350 g potatoes, peeled and cut into chunks

450 g cod or haddock or salmon fillets, or a mixture of all three

250 ml milk

1 large handful flat-leaf parsley, finely chopped

freshly ground black pepper

knob of unsalted butter

plain flour, for coating, seasoned with black pepper

vegetable oil, for frying

for the salsa

½ mango, stoned, peeled, and finely chopped

1 plum tomato, finely chopped

5-cm piece of cucumber, peeled and finely chopped

I have kept the flavours really simple in this recipe, but you could add a variety of ingredients to spice it up – try spring onions, fresh coriander, garlic, chillies, etc., depending on your child's taste. Ella, my eldest daughter, loved a mild Thai green curry at this age, but children's tastes do vary! Serve with a salad or steamed green vegetables.

1 Cook the potatoes in boiling water for 10 minutes until tender.

2 Put the fish into a pan, cover with the milk, and cook gently for about eight to 10 minutes until the fish turns opaque and can be pulled apart in big flakes. Lift the fish out with a slotted spoon, reserving the milk, and flake into a bowl. Check carefully for bones. Add the parsley and season with pepper.

3 Drain the potatoes. Return to the pan and heat gently for a minute to remove any excess water, then mash with butter and a little of the fish milk.

4 Mix the mash with the fish, then shape into about 10 to 15 small rounds. Pat them in seasoned flour to coat both sides, cover, and chill in the fridge for half an hour.

5 Meanwhile, to make the salsa, combine the ingredients in a bowl and set aside.

6 Heat a little oil in a frying pan. Cook the fish cakes on each side for about two to three minutes until golden. Drain on kitchen paper before serving with the salsa.

tomato sauce for spaghetti

makes: 3–4 servings or 2–3 servings plus 1 adult serving

nutrition: vitamins C and E, fibre, and potassium

storage: the sauce can be kept for 3 days in the fridge or up to 3 months in the freezer

12 ripe tomatoes

2 tbsps olive oil

1 clove garlic, finely chopped

100 ml very weak no-salt vegetable stock

small handful of basil leaves, shredded

freshly ground black pepper

150 g spaghetti, to serve

25 g Cheddar or Parmesan cheese, grated, to serve

You can make this sauce with any variety of tomato. Don't worry about irregular shapes or slight blemishes – choose fruit that is firm and has a good tomato aroma. You will need to cut up the spaghetti to help protect your kitchen walls from bright red sauce, or alternatively use baby and toddler pasta shapes!

1 Score a cross in the top of each tomato and put into a heat-proof bowl. Cover with boiling water and leave for one minute. Drain and leave to cool, then peel. Cut the tomatoes into quarters.

2 Heat the oil in a large saucepan, add the garlic, and cook for one minute. Add the tomatoes and vegetable stock to the pan and simmer, uncovered, for about 20 minutes until soft. Add the basil leaves and season to taste with pepper.

3 Whiz the tomato mixture with a hand-held blender or in a food processor or blender, or mash with a potato masher.

4 Bring a large pan of water to the boil and cook the spaghetti according to the packet instructions. To serve, toss the spaghetti in the sauce and sprinkle the cheese on top.

tomato bread soup

12 ripe tomatoes

2 tbsps olive oil

1 clove garlic, finely chopped

100 ml very weak no-salt vegetable stock

4 thick slices of bread

small handful of basil leaves, shredded

freshly ground black pepper

Cheddar or Parmesan cheese, grated, to serve

Follow the method as above to the point where you add the tomatoes and vegetable stock to the pan and simmer uncovered for about 20 minutes until soft. Remove the crusts from the bread and cut into cubes. Stir the bread into the tomato sauce with the basil leaves and season to taste with pepper. Serve the soup with a little cheese sprinkled on top. This is best eaten fresh or stored for a maximum of 24 hours in the fridge (although the bread will become very soft and mushy).

lamb, apricot, & mint burgers

makes: 4 servings plus
1–2 adult servings

nutrition: protein, fibre,
and betacarotene

storage: best eaten fresh or up to
3 months in the freezer

1 tbsp olive oil

2 spring onions, finely sliced

pinch of ground cinnamon

8 mint leaves, finely chopped

500 g lamb mince

6 ready-to-eat dried apricots,
finely chopped

freshly ground black pepper

bread or rolls and salad, to serve

These burgers are quick and easy to make, and they are much tastier than the processed equivalents. Add as much spice, fruit, and herbs as you feel your toddler will enjoy.

1 Heat the oil in a frying pan, add the spring onions, and cook for a few minutes until soft.

2 Add the cinnamon and cook for another couple of minutes. Transfer to a bowl and add the mint, lamb, apricots, and pepper to taste.

3 Mix everything together with your hands, then mould the mixture into about 20 little burgers. If you want to, they can be frozen at this point.

4 Preheat the grill to a high heat. Grill the burgers for about five minutes on each side until cooked through. Serve with bread or rolls and salad.

leek & ham rolls with a cheesy white sauce

makes: 2 servings plus
2 adult servings

nutrition: vitamins A and C, folic
acid, protein, and iron,

storage: 24 hours in the fridge

3 small leeks, washed and trimmed

200 ml milk

20 g plain flour

20 g unsalted butter

freshly ground black pepper

100 g Cheddar cheese, grated

3 thick slices of ham

40 g breadcrumbs

Leeks are highly nutritious and have pronounced antibacterial benefits. This is a perfect Sunday supper dish which is quick, easy, and very tasty.

1 Preheat the oven to 180°C/ 350°F/gas mark 4.

2 Put the leeks in a steamer or in a colander, covered with a lid, over a pan of simmering water and steam for five to 10 minutes until partially cooked. Remove from the heat and allow to cool slightly.

3 Mix together the milk, flour, and butter in saucepan. Heat gently, stirring constantly with a whisk, until you have a smooth sauce.

4 Season with pepper, then add half the cheese and stir until melted.

5 Roll each piece of ham around a leek and transfer to an ovenproof dish. Pour over the cheese sauce and scatter with breadcrumbs and the remaining cheese. Bake in the oven for 20 minutes until cooked through.

tortilla or pitta pizzas

makes: 4 pizzas

nutrition: fibre, vitamin C, potassium, and calcium

storage: best eaten on the day

4 soft flour tortillas or pitta breads

4 tbsps tomato purée

16 cherry tomatoes, cut into quarters

2 avocados

a few black olives, stoned and sliced (optional)

50 g Cheddar cheese, finely grated

Most children love pizzas, but very often they are made with over-processed ingredients. Homemade pizza dough can be quick and simple to make, but this version is even faster. There are lots of different ingredients you can use as toppings; it's a great way to introduce new foods and to encourage your child to eat more vegetables. Try grated courgette and carrot, thin strips of mozzarella, mashed sardines or other fish, pesto, or ham.

1 Preheat the grill to a medium heat.

2 Put the tortillas or pitta breads onto a baking sheet and spread each with a little tomato purée.

3 Top with the tomatoes. Cut the avocados in half and remove the stones. Peel, then thinly slice the flesh and arrange over the bases.

4 Scatter with the sliced olives, if using, and sprinkle the cheese on top. Grill for about five minutes until the cheese has melted and the bases are slightly crisp and golden. Leave to cool slightly, cut into strips to best suit your baby or toddler.

sweet potato frittata

makes: 4 servings or 2 servings plus 1 adult serving

nutrition: protein, vitamins B$_{12}$, C, and E, beta-carotene, and iron

storage: 24 hours in the fridge

150 g sweet potato, peeled and roughly chopped

50 g spinach, washed and destalked

2 tbsps olive oil

½ onion, finely chopped

4 eggs

freshly ground black pepper

organic ketchup and salad, to serve

This has a fabulous sweet flavour and looks pretty, too. Serve in wedges with a mixed salad.

1 Bring a pan of water to the boil, add the sweet potato, and cook for about 10 to 15 minutes until tender.

2 Drain, then whiz with a hand-held blender or in a food processor or blender to a purée.

3 Heat a little water in a pan, add the spinach, and cook for a couple of minutes until wilted. Drain and roughly chop.

4 Heat half the oil in a pan and sauté the onion until soft. Meanwhile, whisk the eggs in a large bowl.

5 Add the onion, puréed sweet potato, and spinach to the eggs. Give it a quick stir without totally blending everything together. Season with pepper.

6 Heat the rest of the oil in a small frying pan, turn the heat down, and pour in the egg mixture. Cook, without stirring, for about five minutes until the egg is almost set.

7 Preheat the grill to a high heat and cook the frittata for one to two minutes until golden brown.

mushroom omelette

makes: 2 servings
nutritional: protein, vitamins A, B$_{12}$, and E, and zinc
storage: best eaten fresh

Omelettes are great breakfast foods, but they will do just as well for lunch or supper. You can make lots of variations; try adding chopped tomato, grated courgette, flaked fish, fresh herbs, grated cheese, or chopped spinach.

2 eggs
1 tbsp milk
freshly ground black pepper
small knob of unsalted butter
1 tsp olive oil
50 g mushrooms, thinly sliced

1 Break the eggs into a bowl with the milk and pepper to taste, and whisk until blended.
2 Heat the butter and oil in a frying pan, add the mushrooms, and cook over a medium heat for about five minutes until golden.

3 Pour in the eggs, tilting the pan to cover the base. Use a wooden spoon to draw the egg from the sides into the middle. Continue until the egg is cooked. Serve immediately.

broad bean & mint dip

makes: 4 servings plus 1–2 adult servings
nutrition: protein, fibre, and betacarotene
storage: best eaten fresh

Broad beans are one of the most nutritionally valuable of all the beans. They are high in protein, which means they are good for vegetarians. If you can't get fresh, use frozen ones – their nutrient quality won't be affected. However, do avoid canned varieties. This is great served with fingers of pitta bread or raw vegetable sticks.

450 g broad beans
handful of mint, finely chopped
1 tbsp lemon juice
1 tbsp olive oil
1 tsp mustard (optional)

1 Bring a small pan of water to the boil, add the beans, and cook for about five minutes until tender. Drain and cool under running water.
2 Remove the skins from the beans and mix with the mint, lemon juice, oil, and mustard, if using. Whiz to a purée with a hand-held blender or in a food processor or blender.

cinnamon & banana porridge

makes: 2–3 servings

nutrition: fibre and energy

storage: 24 hours in the fridge

60 g oats

250 ml milk or soya drink

125 ml boiling water

1 banana, peeled and mashed

pinch of ground cinnamon

This is a great breakfast dish, especially when it's cold outside. It is also good made with dried fruit instead of banana. Try chopped dates, apple, or sultanas.

1 Put the oats, milk or soya drink, and water into a saucepan and bring to the boil.

2 Reduce the heat and simmer gently for five minutes, stirring occasionally, until the porridge is thick and creamy.

3 Add the banana and cinnamon. Mix well and serve.

tropical fruit compote

makes: 3–4 servings plus 1 adult serving

nutrition: vitamin C and folic acid,

storage: 24 hours in the fridge

1 ripe papaya or mango, or use ½ of each

½ small ripe cantaloupe

125 g raspberries

150 ml freshly squeezed apple and raspberry juice, or other mixed juice of your choice

This is a delicious dish for both children and adults. If you have any left over, you can whiz it up to make a smoothie – just add some fruit juice or coconut milk to water it down.

1 Cut the papaya, if using, and melon in half and scoop out and discard the seeds. Peel, then cut the flesh into small pieces. Slice through the mango, if using, either side of the stone. Peel, then cut the flesh into small pieces.

2 Whiz all the fruit with a hand-held blender or in a food processor or blender to a purée. Add the fruit juices and stir well.

fruit smoothies

Fruit smoothies are brilliant for babies and toddlers, providing them with a mixture of vitamins, minerals, and fibre in a very quick and convenient form.

You can make them as thick or thin as you fancy. If you are feeding the smoothie to a baby, whiz the fruit and then add a little liquid to make a fruit purée. For toddlers, add more liquid in the form of milk, soya drink, almond milk (*see* page 67), or water to make a smooth and refreshing drink.

Vary the fruit combinations according to what you have to hand, what's in season, and what your toddler fancies – you can't go far wrong. Using fruit in season will not only be cheaper, but it is also likely to have more flavour and nutritional value than imported produce. For more information about seasonal fruit, take a look at pages 136–7. If you have any leftover smoothies, pour into ice-cube trays and freeze.

Put the prepared fruit into a food processor, blender, or a bowl for a hand-held blender and purée. Add the liquid, e.g. milk, coconut milk, or sparkling water according to taste, and serve.

makes: 2–3 servings plus 1 adult serving

nutrition: vitamin C and fibre

storage: the fruit purée (without the added liquid) can be kept for 48 hours in the fridge or up to 3 months in the freezer

pink smoothie

100 g strawberries, hulled, or raspberries, roughly chopped

1 banana, peeled and roughly chopped

milk, soya drink or almond milk (*see* page 67)

green smoothie

3 kiwi fruits, peeled and roughly chopped

½ green melon, deseeded, peeled, and roughly chopped

still or sparkling mineral water

yellow smoothie

½ mango, stoned, peeled and roughly chopped

1 papaya, deseeded, peeled, and roughly chopped

100 ml coconut milk (do not give nuts to babies if there is any family history of allergies)

blue smoothie (serve immediately)

100 g blueberries

100 g blackberries

1–2 apples, peeled, cored, and roughly chopped

about 150 ml milk or almond milk (*see* page 67)

Your toddler is becoming more independent as he or she develops physically, socially, and emotionally. During this year, toddlers should begin to walk and talk.

It is important to combine emotional and nutritional needs at this stage. Make mealtimes a social event; whenever possible, serve your toddler the same as other family members and encourage everyone to eat and chat together. Celebrate being a family! Be aware that it's not just what your children eat but how they eat that's important. Food can play a major role in the giving and receiving of love and affection, but children should not be made to feel guilty if they eat too much or if they don't finish what's on their plates.

Aim to give toddlers three meals a day, with snacks in between, but don't set yourself hard and fast rules. Some toddlers eat little and often, which ensures an even balance of energy throughout the day. Your child will begin to learn to feed herself, especially if encouraged with finger foods. Self-feeding may turn into a bit of a food fight, but you should let toddlers try at least once a day. Some of my friends have found that a plastic mat placed strategically under the toddler's chair makes mess easier to deal with. Toddlers will also learn to drink from a cup. If you are giving drinks containing sugar – which includes fruit juice – offer them in cups or beakers rather than bottles; the liquid will not stay in contact with the teeth for as long.

1-2 years

Don't make
mealtimes a
battleground.
If there's food left
on the plate, be
laid-back about
it and praise your
child for what
she has eaten.

At this stage, your baby will begin to refuse bottles or will gradually wean herself from the breast during the day. However, toddlers need to be given lots of liquid to make up for this – preferably cooled, boiled water or diluted fruit juices. Bottles should be dispensed with because teats can interfere with speech development. Use cups with spouts, or start to introduce plastic beakers, offering small quantities at a time to help to reduce spillages. It is best to avoid offering any sweet drinks such as squash or fizzy drinks, since first teeth are very susceptible to decay, and the drinks can contribute towards toddler diarrhoea. As soon as teeth appear, encourage twice-daily brushing with a small amount of toothpaste. Aim for this to be an established routine by the time your toddler is two years old. Check with your dentist about the best toothpaste to use – with or without fluoride.

successful feeding

Encourage your child to wash her hands before eating. Also encourage toddlers to drink water with meals; straws can make this more fun. In fact, fun should play a big part at mealtimes. Look for items made with this in mind: baby pasta in funny shapes, brightly coloured plastic spoons, and foods with bright colours and interesting textures, e.g. Salade Niçoise, page 89, and Butternut Squash Risotto, page 94.

Don't make mealtimes a battleground – respect your child's appetite. If there is food left on the plate, be laid-back about it and praise your child for what he or she has eaten. Don't be tempted to offer any alternatives.

your child's diet

planning meals

From the age of one you can offer most food that adults eat – just make sure that it's good quality, fresh, and not heavily processed

Aim to serve your toddler with four servings of starchy foods every day, four servings of fresh fruit and vegetables – preferably locally grown and seasonal to get maximum nutrients from the foods – and one or two servings of meat, fish, or eggs a day.

Use unrefined foods as much as possible, e.g. wholegrain rice and wholemeal bread. They tend to be higher in nutrients.

Food can have much more texture now. In fact, you are unlikely to need the food processor or blender, but food should be cut into bite-sized pieces.

Some shellfish can be introduced in small quantities, e.g. carefully shelled crab or prawns, but watch carefully for any allergic reaction (see page 35).

Don't get too hung up about mess, either; you need to relax about stains on clothes and mess on the floor (it took me a while!) to help your toddler to learn to relax around food too.

Try not to use favourite foods as a bribe or as treats or rewards; otherwise your child will never learn to like "ordinary food". Try not to make a big deal about sweets when your child tries them for the first time; this will just increase their allure. I hardly ever give my daughter Ella sweet foods, although she does still tend to have a slight sweet tooth (maybe it's something to do with the fact that I craved sweet foods during pregnancy).

Cow's milk can now be given as a drink, but milk – whether breast milk, formula, or cow's – should not be taken in large quantities since it can reduce your toddler's appetite. Try to encourage your child to have just one drink at night; this will help with potty-training later. If toddlers have too much to drink before bed, they will be less able to sleep through without wetting themselves.

Continue to give chopped or ground nuts and seeds, if there is no family history of allergies. Whole nuts shouldn't be given until your toddler is able to understand that they must be chewed properly. They can usually manage this when they are about three years old.

Vegetarian toddlers should be eating a couple of servings of vegetarian protein a day, e.g. tofu, beans, pulses, and wholegrains.

Honey can now be introduced gradually, if a little sweetness is needed. Your baby should have about 350 ml of full-fat cow's milk, formula, or breast milk a day.

The following foods should be avoided: sugar – use it only to make sour foods palatable (a little unrefined sugar is much better than using artificial sweetners); salt; tea; and coffee. For more information on foods to avoid, see pages 132–3.

breakfasts

Shakes and smoothies are easy to make in a food processor or blender. You can throw in any fruit, thus encouraging your toddler to choose his or her own concoctions. If you have a juicer, you could also make your own fresh fruit and vegetable juices using a whole variety of combinations.

strawberry & banana thick shake

makes: 2–3 servings

also suitable for: over 8 months, just make half the quantity

nutrition: calcium, protein, and vitamins C and E

storage: best served fresh

125 ml milk or soya drink

2 large handfuls of strawberries, hulled and sliced

60 ml strawberry yogurt

Thick shakes and smoothies are brilliant foods for babies and toddlers, particularly when made with live yogurt, which prevents a build-up of harmful bacteria and yeasts in the gut. You can vary this recipe with almost any fruit or fruit yogurt – look for brands with no added sugar. For older children, try using frozen fruit to make a really thick shake!

Blend all the ingredients together in a food processor or blender, or in a jug with a hand-held blender, until smooth.

mango & raspberry thick shake

makes: 2–3 servings

also suitable for: over 8 months, just make half the quantity

nutrition: calcium, vitamin C, and potassium

storage: best served fresh

125 ml milk or soya drink

½ mango, stoned, peeled, and chopped

2 handfuls of raspberries

50 ml natural yogurt

When shopping for fruit, smell is often your best indication of quality, particularly with mangoes. Look for fruit that gives to gentle pressure and has a lovely, fruity aroma. Mangoes can be quite fibrous, so make sure you blend this shake really well.

Blend all the ingredients together in a food processor or blender, or in a jug with a hand-held blender, until smooth.

egg & spinach florentine

makes: 1 serving

only suitable for: over 1 year

nutrition: protein, B vitamins and vitamin C, iron, and folic acid

storage: best eaten immediately

butter or oil, for greasing

50g fresh (or frozen) spinach, washed and destalked

1 egg

1 tbsp cream

15 g Cheddar cheese, grated

This is a fun way to serve eggs and a great way of incorporating some fresh spinach into your child's diet.

1 Preheat the oven to 180°C/350°F/gas mark 4. Lightly butter or oil a ramekin or small ovenproof dish.
2 If using frozen spinach, squeeze to extract as much liquid as possible. If using fresh spinach, cook with a very little water in a small saucepan until it has just wilted.

3 Finely chop the spinach and put into the ramekin or dish.
4 Make a small hollow in the centre of the spinach and crack the egg into it. Pour on the cream and sprinkle with the cheese.
5 Bake for 10 to 12 minutes, or until the egg is set.

mushrooms & tomatoes on toast

makes: 1 serving

only suitable for: over 1 year

nutrition: minerals, B vitamins, and fibre

storage: best eaten immediately

100 g mushrooms

1 tomato

1 tbsp olive oil

1 tsp chopped parsley

freshly ground black pepper

2 slices wholegrain bread

butter, for spreading

Try using field mushrooms when they are in season, or other more interesting varieties, such as brown cap, oyster, or Portobello. This is also very good served on a granary roll.

1 Wipe the mushrooms clean and cut into bite-sized pieces.
2 Cut the tomato into quarters, remove the seeds, and finely chop.
3 Heat the oil in a pan and fry the mushrooms over a medium-high heat. They will release their juices after a few minutes.

4 Add the tomato and parsley, and heat through. Season with pepper.
5 Meanwhile, toast the bread and spread lightly with butter. Tip the mushroom mixture on top and serve.

lunches

chicken with cheese, bacon, & roasties

makes: 2 servings plus 2 adult servings

nutrition: protein, calcium, B vitamins and vitamin C, and fibre

storage: 24 hours in the fridge

3 boneless, skinless chicken breasts

225 g mozzarella cheese

250 g streaky bacon

handful of basil leaves

for the marinade

2 tbsps lemon juice

2 tbsps olive oil

1½ cloves garlic, chopped

a few sea-salt flakes and freshly ground black pepper

for the roasties

500 g baby new potatoes, scrubbed

2 tbsps olive oil

2 cloves garlic, peeled and finely chopped

a few sprigs of thyme

Chicken is one of the most intensively farmed animals, with routine use of chemically enhanced feed – often fishmeal – and antibiotics. Organic production forbids this. The birds grow at a normal rate and eat a natural diet, which allows a good flavour to develop. Organic chicken pieces can be expensive, so buying a whole bird and jointing it yourself is much more economical. You can use the carcass to make a stock for soups. This is delicious served with spinach.

1 Preheat the oven to 180°C/350°F/gas mark 4.

2 Cut the chicken into small cubes (about nine per breast) and the mozzarella into the same number of cubes. In a bowl, mix together the lemon juice, oil, garlic, and seasoning, then add the chicken. Cover, put into the fridge, and leave to marinate for at least 30 minutes.

3 Meanwhile, put the potatoes into a roasting tin and drizzle with olive oil. Add the garlic and thyme, and roast for 20 to 25 minutes.

4 Stretch the bacon using the back of a knife to make it thin and cut each rasher in half widthways. Arrange the chicken on a baking tray. Cover each piece of chicken with a cube of mozzarella, then a basil leaf, and wrap in a piece of bacon – use wooden cocktail sticks to secure if you fancy (remove before serving).

5 Cook for eight to 10 minutes alongside the potatoes, until the chicken is cooked and the bacon is crisp.

baked tomatoes with cheese

makes: 2–3 servings
also suitable for: over 8 months if cut into small pieces
nutrition: vitamins C and E
storage: best eaten fresh

6 ripe tomatoes
1 tbsp olive oil
1 clove garlic, crushed
large handful of flat-leaf parsley or basil, or a mixture of both, chopped
handful of breadcrumbs
15 g Parmesan or Cheddar cheese, grated

This is a brilliant quick lunch or supper dish, and it's great served on rounds of toast with salad. Choose tomatoes with a good scent – they'll have a much better flavour

1 Preheat the oven to 180°C/350°F/gas mark 4.
2 Slice the tomatoes in half around the middle (unless they are plum tomatoes, which are better sliced in half from the stem). Scoop out the insides and put into a bowl.
3 Heat the oil in a pan and sauté the garlic for a couple of minutes. Add the herbs, breadcrumbs, and tomato flesh. Season with freshly ground black pepper and mix together thoroughly.
4 Stuff the filling into the hollow tomatoes, and sprinkle the tops with a little grated cheese.
5 Bake for 20 minutes, or until brown. Serve on rounds of toast.

bean soup with tomato topping

makes: 2 servings plus 2 adult servings
also suitable for: over 10 months
nutrition: protein, calcium, vitamin C, and fibre
storage: 24 hours in the fridge or up to 3 months in the freezer

for the salsa
3 ripe tomatoes, finely diced
handful of basil leaves, finely chopped
1 tbsp light and fruity olive oil
for the soup
3 tbsps extra-virgin olive oil
2 cloves garlic, finely chopped
small pinch of chilli powder (optional)
400 g can white beans, e.g. cannellini, drained
2 litres vegetable stock
90 g small pasta shapes
Parmesan or Cheddar cheese, grated or shavings, to serve

Beans are great food for toddlers, and are a really good alternative to meat as a source of protein. This soup is ideal for toddlers learning to feed themselves, and it's great for dipping bread into!

1 To make the salsa, mix together the tomatoes, basil, and oil. Put to one side.
2 For the soup, heat the oil in a saucepan, add the garlic and chilli, if using, and cook for a minute or two. Add the beans and stock, and simmer for 15 minutes. Transfer half the soup to a bowl, whiz with a hand-held blender or in a food processor or blender, and return to the pan. Add the pasta and cook, following the packet instructions, until just firm. Season to taste with freshly ground black pepper.
3 Spoon into bowls and sprinkle a little of the tomato salsa and grated cheese over the top.

crunchy avocado salad

makes: 3 servings

only suitable for: over 1 year

nutrition: vitamins C and E, and potassium

storage: 24 hours in the fridge

Ripe avocado has a lovely creamy texture which babies and toddlers love – but it's important that it's fully ripe. This is a great way to incorporate lots of fresh vegetables into your toddler's diet.

2 ripe avocados

a good few squeezes of lime juice

½ red pepper, cored and deseeded

½ cucumber

½ red onion

2 tomatoes, skinned

handful of fresh coriander, chopped

1 tbsp olive oil

1 Cut the avocados in half and remove the stones. Peel, then dice the flesh. Put into a bowl and sprinkle with the lime juice.
2 Dice the pepper, cucumber, onion, and tomatoes. Add to the avocados with the coriander and oil. Mix well. Serve as a filling for pitta bread and/or with vegetable sticks.

salade niçoise

makes: 3–4 servings plus 2 adult servings

also suitable for: over 10 months if eggs are cooked through

nutrition: vitamin C, fibre, protein, and good fatty oils

storage: best eaten immediately

This salad is a mixture of colours, flavours, and textures – perfect for children. You could also use fresh tuna – grill, then flake into large chunks and scatter over the salad.

4 small new potatoes, scrubbed

50 g green beans

2 eggs

100 g mixed baby salad leaves

200 g can tuna, drained

3 medium tomatoes, cut into quarters

50 g black olives, stoned (optional)

2 spring onions, finely sliced

for the dressing

1 tbsp lemon juice

2 tbsps olive oil

1 tbsp finely chopped parsley

1 Cook the potatoes in boiling water for 10 to 15 minutes until tender. Cut into bite-sized pieces.
2 Add the beans to the pan a couple of minutes before the potatoes are cooked, to blanch.
3 Boil the eggs for five to six minutes; the yolks will be soft but not runny. Allow to cool slightly, then peel and cut into quarters.

4 Put the dressing ingredients into a bowl and whisk together. Put all the salad ingredients into a large bowl, drizzle with half the dressing, and serve with more dressing to taste.

suppers

bean & herb sausages with tomato relish

makes: 14 sausages

also suitable for: over 10 months

nutrition: protein, carbohydrates, fibre, B vitamins, iron, and calcium

storage: 3–4 days in the fridge or up to 3 months in the freezer

for the sausages

420 g can baked beans, drained (alternatively, use canned haricot or cannellini beans and add 1 tbsp tomato purée)

100 g soft brown breadcrumbs

45 g medium Cheddar cheese, grated

1 egg, lightly beaten

1 small onion, finely chopped

1 tbsp chopped herbs of your choice, e.g. thyme or parsley

1 tbsp lemon juice

freshly ground black pepper

for the coating

dried breadcrumbs

vegetable oil, for frying

for the tomato relish

200 g tomatoes, very finely chopped

¼ red onion, very finely chopped

½ clove garlic, crushed

¼ red pepper, cored, deseeded, and very finely chopped

2 tbsps olive oil

2 tsps red-wine vinegar

This dish is especially good for vegetarians, who rely on beans as a major source of protein. Look out for baked beans that contain lower amounts of added salt and sugar than conventional canned varieties. These sausages are good served with bread and butter and salad.

1 Put the beans into a bowl and mash with a fork. Add the rest of the sausage ingredients and mix together thoroughly. Form the mixture into approximately 18 to 20 sausages about 10 cm long.

2 Roll the sausages in the dried breadcrumbs, cover, and chill in the fridge for 30 minutes.

3 Meanwhile, to make the relish, mix all the ingredients together in a bowl, cover, and refrigerate.

4 Heat the oil in a frying pan and cook the sausages for two to three minutes before turning, then cook for another six to eight minutes, turning frequently to ensure that they brown evenly. Drain on kitchen paper and serve with the relish.

italian pasta

makes: 4–5 servings

also suitable for: over 10 months

nutrition: vitamins C and E, fibre, and carbohydrates

storage: 2 days in fridge or up to 3 months in the freezer

1 tbsp olive oil

1 onion, chopped

1 clove garlic, chopped

2 tbsps tomato purée

450 g fresh tomatoes, finely chopped

a few basil leaves, finely chopped

a few black olives, stoned and chopped (optional)

freshly ground black pepper

275 g pasta shapes or spaghetti

This sauce is a great freezer stand-by, and can be served with noodles, rice, polenta or even just plain old mashed potato, as well as pasta. Pasta is a great food for toddlers, and small pasta shapes are ideal for encouraging your child to chew. To make it a bit more substantial, try adding a small tin of flaked tuna at the end.

1 Heat the oil in a saucepan, add the onion and garlic, and cook for five to 10 minutes. Add the tomato purée and tomatoes, and cook for another 10 minutes. Add the basil and olives, if using, and season with pepper.

2 Meanwhile, bring a pan of water to the boil, add the pasta, and cook according to the packet instructions.

3 Whiz the tomato mixture with a hand-held blender or in a food processor or blender. Return to the pan and keep warm until needed. Serve with the pasta shapes or spaghetti.

crispy chicken fingers

makes: 2 servings

also suitable for: over 10 months

nutrition: protein, vitamin B_{12}, iron, and zinc

storage: do not reheat but they can be eaten cold the next day

125g low-salt or unsalted crisps

2 boneless, skinless chicken breasts

3 tbsps tomato ketchup

Try to get crisps with very little added salt. This is a quick and easy way to cook and eat chicken – kids love it – and it's good served with steamed green vegetables and mashed potatoes.

1 Preheat the oven to 180°C/ 350°F/gas mark 4.

2 Crush the crisps into small pieces while they are still in the bag, then tip into a bowl.

3 Cut the chicken breasts into bite-sized fingers. Put them into a bowl with the ketchup and mix until they are coated in it.

4 Dip the chicken fingers into the broken crisps. Put onto a baking tray and bake for five to 10 minutes, until cooked through and crispy on the outside.

sausage pie

makes: 2–3 servings plus 1–2 adult servings

nutrition: protein, fibre, and vitamins

storage: up to two months in the freezer

2 medium potatoes, peeled

1 tbsp olive oil

4 sausages

1 small onion, finely chopped

1 small garlic clove, crushed (optional)

1 leek, diced

2 carrots, peeled and diced

1 parsnip, peeled and diced

1 tbsp chopped parsley

200 ml tomato passata

50 g Cheddar cheese, grated

Choose good-quality pork sausages – try some with leeks or herbs, or vegetarian sausages if you prefer. Cut the vegetables into small cubes to make the food easy for your toddler to eat.

1 Preheat the oven to 200°C/ 400°F/gas mark 6.

2 Cook the potatoes in boiling water until just tender. Drain, then slice thinly.

3 Meanwhile, heat the oil in a pan and fry the sausages for about 10 minutes, until golden brown.

4 Remove the sausages from the pan and add the onion and garlic. Sauté until soft.

5 Add the leek, carrots, and parsnip, and cook for another two to three minutes.

6 Add the parsley, passata, and 100 ml boiling water, and bring to the boil.

7 Slice each sausage into three and arrange in an ovenproof dish. Pour on the vegetable mixture and top with the potato slices. Cover with foil and bake for 35 minutes.

8 Remove the foil and sprinkle with the cheese. Bake for a further 20 minutes.

chicken patties

makes: 6 patties

also suitable for: over 10 months

nutrition: protein and B vitamins

storage: up to 24 hours in the fridge

2 skinless, boneless chicken breasts

2 tbsps breadcrumbs

1 egg, beaten

2 tbsps chopped parsley or chives

1 tbsp Greek yogurt

4 spring onions, finely chopped

1 small clove garlic, crushed (optional)

for the sauce

4 tbsps Greek yogurt

1 tbsp finely chopped mixed herbs

1 tsp mild grainy mustard

These are great served hot or cold. They can be served in buns or pitta bread with salad or green vegetables. Instead of the yogurt sauce you could serve them with a fruity salsa (*see* page 71) or some ketchup.

1 Roughly chop the chicken. Put it into a food processor and whiz until minced.

2 Add the breadcrumbs, egg, herbs, yogurt, spring onions, garlic, if using, and freshly ground black pepper to taste. Whiz again until well mixed.

3 Turn into a bowl and shape into balls, then pat each one down to make a patty – try wetting your hands a little if the mixture is sticky. Cover and chill in the fridge for 15 minutes.

3 Preheat the grill to a medium heat. Cook the patties for about 10 minutes, turning occasionally, until cooked through. Meanwhile, mix all the sauce ingredients together in a small bowl.

4 Serve the patties hot or cold with the sauce.

butternut squash risotto

makes: 2–3 servings plus 1–2 adult servings

nutrition: protein, vitamin C, and calcium

storage: rice should not be reheated but can be chilled for up to 24 hours and served at room temperature

25 g butter

1 tbsp olive oil

3 shallots, chopped finely

½ butternut squash, chopped into 1 cm cubes

175 g arborio rice

600 ml weak low-salt vegetable stock

4 tbsps chopped fresh coriander

25 g Parmesan or Cheddar cheese, grated

freshly ground black pepper

This quantity is enough for adults as well as little ones. Alternatively, halve the mixture and serve to just toddlers. Stock cubes are best made weaker than recommended. Use just half a cube to the required quantity of water.

1 Preheat the oven to 180°C/350°F/gas mark 4.

2 Melt the butter with the oil in a heavy-based pan and fry the shallots and squash slowly, for five to 10 minutes, until softened. Turn the heat up slightly and add the rice to the pan. Stir thoroughly, coating with the buttery shallots, for a minute or two until you hear the rice make a hissing sound, which means it is now time to add the liquid.

3 Add a ladleful of the stock, let that bubble, and then add the remaining stock and one tablespoon of the coriander. Bring up to simmering point. Stir once and transfer to a warm ovenproof dish. Cook, uncovered, on the middle shelf of the oven.

4 After 15 minutes, remove from the oven and stir once. Return to the oven for a further 10 to 15 minutes. Finally, when the risotto is ready, remove from the oven and stir in the cheese and the remaining chopped coriander. Season with pepper and leave to stand for a couple of minutes before serving.

plaice with a nutty stuffing

makes: 4 servings plus 2 adult servings

nutrition: B vitamins and vitamins D and C, protein, zinc, and energy

storage: best eaten fresh or up to 3 months in the freezer

700 g plaice or sole fillets, skinned

500 g potatoes, well-scrubbed but not peeled

2 tbsps olive oil

1 tsp paprika

steamed baby spinach and green beans and chunks of lemon, to serve

for the stuffing

50 g pine nuts (do not give nuts to toddlers if there is any family history of allergies)

50 g walnuts (do not give nuts to toddlers if there is any family history of allergies)

1 onion, finely chopped

4 cloves garlic, chopped

3 handfuls fresh coriander, chopped

2 tsps each ground cumin, ground coriander, and paprika

zest of 1 lemon

2 tbsps olive oil

This is a really easy dish to prepare and great for adults too. If you cannot get good fresh fish, use frozen. In fact, frozen fish is a great freezer standby. It's usually ready-prepared, so it's very simple to cook. Try steaming it with some fresh herbs for a super-fast meal. Many of the nutrients in potatoes are in their skins, so I have left them on, although any chemical residues will also be found in the skin, so you may wish to buy organic.

1 Preheat the oven to 190°C/375°F/gas mark 5.

2 To make the stuffing, dry-fry the nuts in a frying pan until golden. Cool, then finely chop and put into a food processor. Add the remaining stuffing ingredients and whiz to a rough powder.

3 Lay a plaice fillet on a board, sprinkle with some of the filling, roll up the fillet, and secure with a wooden cocktail stick. Transfer to a plate. Repeat with the other fillets, cover, and chill until needed.

4 Cut the potatoes into little chunks.

5 Heat the oil in a roasting tin. Add the potatoes and paprika, and mix together so that the potatoes are well coated. Roast for 10 to 15 minutes. Give the potatoes another good mix.

6 Add the plaice rolls to the roasting tin and cook with the potatoes for 10 to 15 minutes. Serve the plaice and potatoes with a few lightly steamed green vegetables and lemon chunks.

chicken & fruit pilaf

makes: 2 servings plus
2 adult servings

also suitable for: over 10 months

nutrition: protein, iron, potassium,
folic acid, fibre, and carbohydrate

storage: rice should not be reheated
but can be served cold
up to 24 hours

1 tbsp olive oil

1 shallot, finely chopped

1 clove garlic, finely chopped

4 ready-to-eat dried apricots,
roughly chopped

40 g raisins

3 fresh Medjool dates, stoned and
roughly chopped

150 g basmati rice

300 ml weak low-salt vegetable stock

2 tsps olive oil

3 boneless, skinless chicken breasts

1 tbsp flat-leaf parsley, chopped

I have made a large quantity of this to serve a couple of adults as well as the toddlers. If you want less, just halve the ingredients, but cook the rice for the same amount of time. Don't be tempted to reheat rice; it is a common cause of food poisoning.

1 Preheat the oven to 180°C/350°F/gas mark 4.

2 Heat the oil in a saucepan, add the shallot, and cook gently for five to 10 minutes until soft. Add the garlic and fruit, and cook gently for one to two minutes. Add the rice and stock, cover, and bring to the boil.

3 Reduce the heat without removing the lid and simmer for 14 minutes. Remove from the heat and leave to stand for 10 minutes.

4 While the rice is cooking, drizzle a little oil over the chicken breasts. Put into a shallow roasting tin and cook in the oven for 10 to 15 minutes. Season the rice and add the parsley. Slice the chicken thinly and mix through the rice.

treats

raspberry & banana crumble

Crumbles are a favourite treat with children and are very easy to make. You can use almost any combination of fruit – look for what's in season (*see* pages 134–5).

makes: 6 servings

also suitable for: over 10 months

nutrition: potassium, vitamin C, fibre, and vitamin A

storage: 24 hours in the fridge or up to 3 months in the freezer

1 banana

450 g fresh or frozen raspberries

a drizzle of honey (optional)

for the crumble topping

70 g unsalted butter

75 g wholemeal flour, or a mixture of plain and wholemeal

50 g dessicated coconut

50 g oats

25 g finely chopped hazelnuts

1 tsp ground cinnamon

1 Preheat the oven to 180°C/ 350°F/gas mark 4.

2 Peel and chop the banana into small pieces. Put into an ovenproof dish with the raspberries. Drizzle with the honey, if using (if the raspberries are sweet, you probably won't need it).

3 To make the crumble, rub the butter into the flour. Mix in the coconut, oats, hazelnuts (remember – do not give nuts to toddlers if there is any family history of allergies), and cinnamon. Scatter over the fruit and bake for 25 to 30 minutes.

peanut butter eggy bread

Try to avoid factory-made bread if you can, and choose organic loaves made by a baker. If you do buy pre-packaged bread, check that it is completely organic, not just made with organic flour. This eggy bread is also delicious served with bacon, or for a more healthy option, with green salad.

Makes: 4 slices bread

Nutritional: a good source of protein and fibre, B vitamins

Storage: best eaten immediately

4 tbsps (approx) smooth peanut butter (do not give nuts to toddlers if there is any family history of allergies)

4 slices wholemeal bread

1 egg

100 ml milk or soya drink

20g butter and 1 tbsp vegetable oil

1 Spread the peanut butter on one side of each of the slices of bread.

2 Mix egg and milk together in a shallow dish. Dip the bread into the eggy mixture.

3 Heat the oil and butter in a pan and fry the dipped bread, turning over after two to three minutes, so that each side is golden brown. Serve immediately.

fruity yogurt bars

makes: 8 bars

also suitable for: over 10 months

nutrition: fibre, protein, and betacarotene

storage: 1 week in an airtight container or up to 3 months in the freezer

These are really quick to make and children love them. For those who don't like apricots, use 125 g grated apple instead – the bars will be slightly squidgier but just as delicious!

75g self-raising flour

50g oats

25 g unsweetened desiccated coconut (do not give nuts to toddlers if there is any family history of allergies)

25 g unrefined, soft brown sugar

50 g prunes, finely chopped

125 g ready-to-eat dried apricots, finely chopped

50 g unsalted butter

50 g natural yogurt

1 Preheat the oven to 180°C/ 350°F/gas mark 4.

2 Put all the dry ingredients into a large bowl. Melt the butter and pour into the bowl with the yogurt. Mix everything together thoroughly.

3 Press into a loaf tin and smooth the top down. Bake in the oven for 25 minutes. Leave to cool before cutting into bars.

pumpkin fritters

makes: 18 fritters

also suitable for: over 10 months without the sugar to serve

nutrition: potassium, vitamin C, protein, and fibre

storage: 48 hours in the fridge

These are like little pancakes rather than greasy, deep-fried fritters, and toddlers love them. They are delicious with cinnamon and a little sugar – it sounds like an odd combination but it really works!

350 g pumpkin or butternut squash

6 tbsps plain flour

2 tsps baking powder

1 egg

vegetable oil and butter, for frying

a little golden caster sugar and ground cinnamon, to serve

1 Peel the pumpkin or squash, remove the seeds, and cut the flesh into small chunks.

2 Bring a pan of water to the boil, add the pumpkin or squash, and simmer for 15 to 20 minutes until very soft. Drain well and whiz with a hand-held blender or in a food processor or blender to make a purée.

3 Add the flour, baking powder, and egg, and whiz again until combined. Heat a little oil and

butter in a heavy-based frying pan. When very hot, drop spoonfuls of the batter into the pan.

4 Lower the heat to medium. Cook the fritters for two to three minutes. When little air bubbles start to show on the surface, flip them over with a palette knife and cook for a further two to three minutes.

5 Transfer to a cooling rack covered in kitchen paper to absorb any fat. Serve with a sprinkling of sugar and cinnamon.

creamy banana ice

makes: 3–4 servings

also suitable for: over 10 months in small quantities

nutrition: potassium, vitamin A, fibre, and starch

storage: do not refreeze; up to 3 months in the freezer

3 very ripe bananas

This is a great easy pudding for children, especially in the summer. They love the creamy, ice-cream-like texture. You could add some other soft fruit, such as blueberries, finely chopped strawberries, or passion-fruit pulp for a bit of variety. Bananas are excellent for the digestion.

1 Peel, then mash the bananas in a bowl and transfer to a small freezerproof container.

2 Cover and freeze for several hours or overnight.

3 Before serving, remove from the freezer and leave to stand for five minutes. Using a fork, beat the banana until light and creamy. Serve immediately.

popcorn

makes: 3 servings

also suitable for: over 10 months

nutrition: fibre and protein

storage: best eaten fresh

1 tbsp olive oil

60 g popcorn

This is a brilliant snack. Rather than adding sugar or salt, add other things to jazz it up – try cinnamon, toasted sesame seeds, or a drizzle of honey.

1 Heat the oil in a deep saucepan and add the kernels. Cover tightly and cook over a medium heat, shaking occasionally. You will hear the popcorn start to pop.

2 Only remove the lid when there are no more pops. Leave to cool slightly, then sprinkle with your chosen topping and serve.

mini-muffins

makes: 16

also suitable for: over 10 months

nutrition: vitamin C, fibre, and calcium

storage: 2–3 days in an airtight container or up to 3 months in the freezer

These are brilliant for children. They can easily be made savoury if you prefer – omit the sugar and add other ingredients of your choice, e.g. sweetcorn, grated Cheddar or other cheese, chopped herbs, chopped olives, or sun-dried tomatoes. Muffin cases are available from most supermarkets; they make washing-up a little easier and keep the muffins fresher for longer.

185 g plain flour

1 tsp baking powder

1 tsp bicarbonate of soda

80 g golden caster sugar

1 egg, beaten

125 ml milk

3 tbsps melted butter

150 g chopped fruit, e.g. banana or blueberries, and finely chopped nuts, e.g. hazelnuts or almonds

1 Preheat the oven to 200°C/400°F/gas mark 6. Butter mini-muffin tins.
2 Sift the flour, baking powder, and bicarbonate of soda into a bowl. Make a well in the centre. Add the remaining ingredients, gently folding everything together to make a wet batter.

3 Spoon the batter into the buttered tins.
4 Bake for about 12 minutes, or until golden brown and firm to the touch.

tomato & buttermilk scones

makes: 20 little scones

also suitable for: over 10 months occasionally

nutrition: protein, calcium, and potassium

storage: 4 days in an airtight container or up to 3 months in the freezer

Scones are really quick and easy to make, and they freeze brilliantly. They make appealing snacks – particularly if you buy some small or fun-shaped cutters. Try the different suggested flavourings for variety.

450 g self-raising flour

60 g butter

50 g sun-dried tomatoes, finely chopped

1 tbsp chopped parsley

284 ml carton buttermilk

1 Preheat the oven to 180°C/350°F/gas mark 4.
2 Sieve the flour into large bowl, then rub in the butter. Stir in the tomatoes and parsley, then add enough buttermilk to make a soft, sticky dough.
3 Tip the dough out onto a floured surface and knead lightly until smooth. Pat the dough out to a 2-cm thickness and cut into shapes as desired.
4 Put the scones onto a greased baking tray. Bake for 10 minutes

until risen and golden. Leave to cool on a wire rack.

variations

Use grated cheese with sesame seeds and poppy seeds in place of the tomatoes and parsley. For sweet scones, use one teaspoon golden icing sugar, unsweetened desiccated coconut, and chopped dried fruit instead of the tomatoes and parsley.

blueberry & banana pancakes

makes: 12–14 pancakes

also suitable for: over 10 months occasionally

nutrition: vitamin C, fibre, and calcium

storage: best eaten fresh or up to 1 month in the freezer

1 egg
284 ml carton buttermilk
15 g unsalted butter, melted
60 g unbleached white flour
60 g wholemeal flour
1 tsp bicarbonate of soda
1 large banana, peeled and diced
100 g blueberries
1 tsp vegetable oil

These are truly delicious served with more fresh fruit or a tiny drizzle of honey.

1 In a bowl, whisk together the egg, buttermilk, and melted butter.
2 In a separate bowl, combine the dry ingredients. Make a well in the centre and pour in the buttermilk mixture. Using a wooden spoon, stir the buttermilk mixture until the dry ingredients are incorporated.
3 Stir the fruit into the batter. Heat a heavy-based frying pan with the vegetable oil, then reduce to a medium heat.
4 Spoon three tablespoons of the batter for each pancake into the pan. Cook for about two to three minutes until air bubbles appear on the top of the pancakes, then flip them over with a palette knife. Cook for another minute or two until lightly browned.
5 Keep warm in a low oven on sheets of greaseproof paper while you cook the others. If you freeze them, put greaseproof paper between the layers. After defrosting, gently warm them in a low oven.

pitta bread crisps

makes: about 20

nutrition: carbohydrate, protein, and calcium

storage: best eaten immediately

2 pitta breads
2 tbsps olive oil
40 g mozzarella cheese, grated
35 g Cheddar cheese, grated
1 tbsp chopped parsley

This is a super-quick, tasty treat. These crisps are also great served with soup or with raw vegetables sticks.

1 Preheat the grill to a medium heat. Split the pitta breads through the middle lengthways and open out so that you have two pieces of thin bread. Cut each piece into strips or triangles.
2 Arrange in a single layer on a large baking tray. Grill the pittas until they start to crisp and turn golden.
3 Drizzle with the oil and sprinkle with the cheeses. Return to the grill for a few minutes until the cheese is melted and golden.
4 Leave to cool slightly before serving sprinkled with parsley.

Your baby will change enormously during this stage. He will still be growing rapidly, and at around two-and-a-half years old will have a full set of primary teeth.

At the beginning of this stage toddlers will be able to feed themselves with a spoon, and by the age of three, they may be able to start using a knife and fork. With their new-found confidence, they will start to be more choosy about what they eat and will become more particular about food. This making of choices, however irrational it may seem, is very important, because it is a way of asserting their independence. You may also notice a slight reduction in appetite.

Toddlers have new skills, which will make them more independent, but they will still rely on you for lots of other things. This can result in many confrontations, especially at mealtimes, which can be a challenge for both toddler and parent. To make life easier, establish some ground rules and be consistent: your child needs to know what you will and won't tolerate.

Encourage your child to think of mealtimes as an adventure. I once gave my eldest daughter, Ella, chopsticks to eat a stir-fry with and she loved it (although most of the food was eaten with her fingers!). Also, by involving your child in food preparation, you can make meals an opportunity for learning as well – baking is an activity that toddlers really do seem to enjoy.

2-3 years

Explain to your child why you choose certain foods and not others to help him understand your reasoning.

You will find that your toddler is becoming more independent as he starts to chat and toddle around. Toddlers can get up from the table when they choose, and you will notice that they have specific likes and dislikes. By now, you should have laid the foundations of good eating habits, on which you can continue to build. However, you may no longer have complete control over what your child is eating and drinking.

It is very likely that he will be interacting with more people now, at nursery school, friends' houses, parties, etc., and may well be influenced by others and the foods they are eating. If avoiding certain foods is out of your control – for example, eating biscuits at nursery – do not offer them at home.

successful feeding

Be guided by your toddler's appetite rather than by someone telling you exactly how much he should be eating.

Explain to your child why you choose certain foods and not others to help him understand your reasoning. Teach healthy eating – you can't rely on the education system to do this. Allow plenty of time for meals and discourage fast eating, which can result in indigestion problems in later life.

Breakfast is the most important meal of the day. Avoid giving cereals with lots of added sugar – they are often high in salt, too. Porridge or oat-based cereals are best, since they are high in complex carbohydrates which release energy over several hours, setting toddlers up for the day. You can serve them with either fresh or dried fruit.

your child's diet

Try to avoid convenience foods. Most are over-processed, lacking in nutrients, and full of additives. There are lots of fresh foods that can be made into meals just as quickly. Try cheese on toast, garlic bread with tomatoes, or peanut butter eggy bread, page 98.

planning meals

Your toddler should be eating three regular meals a day, plus healthy snacks to help keep energy levels high and constant. Avoid giving snacks too close to mealtimes, since this may reduce appetites.

A well-balanced diet is essential for your toddler's healthy develop- ment, so include as broad a range of foods as you can (see page 8).

Try to limit sweet foods. If they are not part of day-to-day life, toddlers are less likely to crave them or develop a sweet tooth. Sweet foods can also contribute to conditions such as tooth decay, diabetes, weight-related disorders, and irritable bowel. It is much

better to offer naturally sweet food such as fresh or dried fruit or healthy sweet treats: *see* pages 120–9.

Don't get into the habit of always offering desserts, regardless of how healthy they are. If your toddler always ends a meal with something sweet, it can become a habit for life. Instead, you could offer a light starter, seconds of the main course, or something savoury afterwards – perhaps cheese with crackers or bread.

Serve raw fruit and vegetables as much as possible; they are higher in nutrients than when cooked. This practice also develops your child's taste for healthy food. If your child is not a big vegetable fan, try juicing them instead. Mixing a little sweet juice with savoury also makes juices more popular; try apple and celery or pineapple, ginger, and carrot.

Your baby should be drinking about 350 ml of cow's milk or

formula a day. Skimmed cow's milk should not be given, but semi-skimmed is acceptable if your child is a good eater and consuming a varied diet. The following foods should be avoided: sugar – use it only to make sour foods palatable; salt; tea; and coffee. If there is any history of allergy in your family, avoid nuts and foods containing nuts. For more information about foods to avoid, *see* pages 132–3.

breakfasts

crispy potato pancakes

makes: 10 pancakes

also suitable for: over 10 months cut into small pieces (depending on topping)

nutrition: carbohydrates, vitamin C, and protein

storage: 48 hours in the fridge

550 g potatoes, peeled and halved

2 eggs, beaten

3 tbsps plain flour

1 small onion, finely chopped

grating of nutmeg (optional)

freshly ground black pepper

2 tbsps olive oil

These are delicious for all the family. They can be served on their own or with lots of different toppings. Try a tiny knob of butter or some ketchup. For a more substantial breakfast or lunch dish, try serving them with one of the suggested toppings.

1 Fill a large saucepan with cold water, add the potatoes, and bring to the boil. Cook for five minutes until parboiled. Drain, cool, and grate coarsely. Put onto kitchen paper to soak up excess water.

2 In a bowl, combine the potato, eggs, flour, onion, nutmeg, if using, and pepper to taste. Mix them until well combined.

3 Heat a heavy-based frying pan, add half the oil, and drop in spoonfuls of the pancake mixture. Cook for about two to three minutes on each side. Repeat with the remaining oil and pancake mixture.

suggested toppings

poached eggs, wilted spinach, crispy bacon, grilled tomatoes

crunchy fruity cereal

makes: lots of servings!

nutrition: protein, fibre, calcium, potassium, and vitamin C

storage: 2 weeks in airtight container

250 g oats

40 g each of wheat germ, unsweetened desiccated coconut, chopped sesame and sunflower seeds

75 g nuts, finely chopped (do not give nuts to toddlers if there is any family history of allergies)

100 ml olive oil

50 ml runny honey

a few drops of vanilla extract

150 g mixed dried fruit

This is really easy to make and much better for your child than ordinary breakfast cereals, which are packed with sugar, salt, and additives. You can make different kinds by just changing the type of fruit and nuts you add. It is especially good served with yogurt or fresh fruit. You could also use it as a crumble topping for fruit.

1 Preheat the oven to 150°C/ 300°F/gas mark 2.

2 Grease a large baking tray. In a large bowl, mix together the oats, wheat germ, coconut, sesame seeds, sunflower seeds, and nuts.

3 In a large saucepan, combine the oil, honey, and vanilla. Heat gently until the honey has melted.

4 Pour the honey mixture over the dry ingredients and mix thoroughly. Spread the mixture out in the greased tray.

5 Bake for 35 to 40 minutes, stirring every 10 minutes.

6 Remove from the oven and leave to cool completely. Break up any large pieces and add the fruit.

lunches

zesty chicken with mango

makes: 2–3 servings

also suitable for: over 10 months if cut into small pieces and in small quantities

nutrition: protein, vitamin C, and good fatty oils

storage: 24 hours in the fridge

3 skinless, boneless chicken breasts

1 large ripe mango

1 large avocado

for the dressing

2 tbsps olive oil

1 tbsp citrus-fruit juice, e.g. orange or lime juice

freshly ground black pepper

I thought I would include a recipe for poached chicken because the end result is so tender and juicy – a texture your toddler should love. Alternatively, if time is short, you could sauté the chicken.

1 Pour about 5 cm of water into a shallow frying pan.

2 Add the chicken breasts and cook over a high heat for two minutes on each side.

3 Lower the heat to a simmer, cover the pan, and cook the chicken for a further two minutes. Remove the pan from the heat and leave to stand, covered, for about five minutes until the chicken is firm to the touch.

4 Remove from the water and leave to cool for a few minutes before transferring to a bowl. Cover and chill in the fridge for 30 minutes.

5 Slice through the mango either side of the stone. Peel, then cut the flesh into slices.

6 Halve the avocado and remove the stone. Peel, then slice the flesh into strips.

7 Cut the cooled chicken into thin slices and put into a bowl. Add the mango and avocado, and mix everything together.

8 Mix the dressing ingredients together, season with a little pepper, and drizzle over the chicken, mango, and avocado.

beef satay sticks

makes: 5–6 sticks

nutrition: protein, potassium, and niacin

storage: 2 days in the fridge

175 g beef or lamb fillet or 2 small chicken breasts

for the sauce

6 tbsps crunchy or smooth peanut butter (do not give nuts to toddlers if there is any family history of allergies)

2 tbsps lemon juice

1 tsp reduced-salt light soy sauce

2 tbsps boiling water

Remove the meat from the sticks before serving to toddlers. Children love peanut butter and this is a brilliant way to use it. You can serve the satay with rice and green vegetables such as mange-tout, or serve cold with a salad of bean sprouts, grated carrot, and cucumber.

1 Preheat the grill to a medium heat.

2 Cut the meat into bite-sized pieces. Mix together all the sauce ingredients and stir in the meat pieces, making sure that they are well-coated.

3 Thread onto skewers and grill for 10 to 15 minutes, or until the meat is cooked through.

nutty apple coleslaw

makes: 4–5 servings

nutrition: vitamins A, C, and E, folic acid, potassium, and fibre

storage: 24 hours (undressed) in the fridge

½ small red cabbage, shredded

½ small white cabbage, shredded

2 celery sticks, finely sliced

2 red apples, cored and coarsely grated

40 g cheese, grated or chopped

3 tbsps each sesame and sunflower seeds, toasted (do not give nuts to toddlers if there is any family history of allergies)

for the dressing

3 tbsps natural yogurt

½ clove garlic, crushed

3 tsps lemon juice

1 tbsp finely chopped mint

1 tsp runny honey

This coleslaw is lovely served with cold chicken or ham, especially in sandwiches.

In a bowl, combine the cabbages, celery, apples, cheese, and seeds. For the dressing, combine all the ingredients and mix well. When ready to serve, combine the two.

quick tomato & pasta

makes: 3–4 servings

also suitable for: over 10 months

nutrition: carbohydrate, calcium, and vitamins C and E

storage: 24 hours in the fridge

3 handfuls baby pasta, e.g. stars or hoops

4 ripe plum or 2 large beef tomatoes, finely chopped

60 g mozzarella cheese, in small pieces

large handful of baby spinach leaves

8 or 10 basil leaves, finely shredded

1 tbsp olive oil

30 g pine nuts, toasted (optional) and finely chopped (do not give nuts to toddlers if there is any family history of allergies)

To make this more of a meal in one, you could add some sliced cold chicken or grilled bacon. Serve with some bread to mop up all the tomato juices.

1 Bring a saucepan of water to the boil and cook the pasta according to the packet instructions. Drain.

2 While still warm, add the tomatoes, mozzarella, spinach, basil, and olive oil, and combine.

3 Serve with a sprinkling of pine nuts.

fruity carrots

makes: 3–4 servings

nutrition: betacarotene and vitamins A and C

storage: 24 hours (undressed) in the fridge

1 orange

2 carrots, scrubbed and grated

100 g raisins

1 tbsp poppy seeds

1 handful watercress

for the dressing

juice of 1 orange

2 tbsps olive oil

pinch of dry English mustard

Mixing carrots with something sweet, such as oranges, and with nuts, to add texture, is a great way to encourage children to eat more vegetables. If using organic carrots there is no need to peel them, particularly since there is a high concentration of nutrients in the skin; just give them a good scrub and then grate them.

1 To prepare the orange, slice off the top and bottom. Then, using a serrated knife, cut away the peel from the sides, turning the orange around as you go. Holding the orange over a bowl to catch the juice, cut out the segments from between the membranes.

2 Add the carrots, raisins, poppy seeds, and watercress to the orange segments and juice. Mix together gently.

3 Whisk together all the dressing ingredients in a small bowl and pour over the salad.

suppers

all-in-one chicken casserole

makes: 4 servings

nutrition: vitamins B$_{12}$ and C, iron, zinc, and fibre

storage: best eaten fresh (do not reheat rice)

2 tbsps olive oil

6 chicken thighs or chicken pieces, seasoned with freshly ground black pepper

1 onion, finely chopped

2 carrots, diced

200 g basmati or other long-grain rice

3 large vine tomatoes, chopped

450 ml chicken stock (very weak if using cubes)

150 g green beans, chopped

small handful of herbs, chopped

This is a great all-in-one dish which really saves on the washing-up! With chicken (and eggs), the term "free-range" actually means very little. Poultry is often raised in a similar way to standard birds, with just a little more space and outside access, but no difference in feed or welfare. You may wish to choose organic chicken.

1 Preheat the oven to 200°C/400°F/gas mark 6.

2 Heat half the oil in frying pan, add the chicken, and brown all over. Transfer to a plate.

3 Heat the remaining oil and sauté the onion for a few minutes until soft. Add the carrots and rice, and stir-fry for a few minutes.

4 Spoon the rice into the bottom of a small casserole dish. Top with the chopped tomatoes and chicken. Season with freshly ground black pepper. Pour in the stock, cover, and bake for 20 minutes.

5 Remove from the oven and stir in the beans and herbs.

6 Return to the oven and cook for a further 10 minutes, or until the chicken and rice are cooked through.

noodles with tofu & vegetables

makes: 4 servings

nutrition: protein, vitamin C, betacarotene, iron, fibre, and potassium

storage: best served fresh

2 tbsps reduced-salt soy sauce

1 clove garlic, finely chopped

2 tsps grated fresh root ginger

2 tbsps olive oil

200 g firm tofu, drained and diced

200 g noodles

½ red pepper, cored, deseeded, and finely sliced

½ head broccoli, cut into tiny florets

75 g frozen sweetcorn

juice of ½ lime

freshly ground black pepper

Soya products made from soya protein isolates may be heavily treated with chemicals. Many soya beans are also genetically modified, especially those from the USA. Buying soya products made from whole soya beans which are organic is the only way to avoid this. Tofu is a great source of protein for vegetarians and vegans.

1 Mix together the soy sauce, garlic, ginger, and one tablespoon of the oil.

2 Add the diced tofu to the mixture and mix well. Cover and refrigerate for at least one hour, preferably overnight.

3 Bring a large pan of water to the boil, add the noodles, and cook according to the packet instructions. Drain.

4 Heat the remaining one tablespoon of oil in a wok, add the pepper, broccoli, sweetcorn, and tofu, and stir-fry for a few minutes.

5 Reduce the heat, cover with a lid, and "steam" for a few minutes until warmed through. Add the noodles and toss everything together. Add the lime juice and season with pepper to taste.

felafel with minty yogurt

makes: about 12 felafel

also suitable for: over 10 months in small quantities and if chopped very finely

nutrition: energy, iron, potassium, and protein

storage: best eaten fresh, although they will keep for 24 hours in the fridge

2 x 400 g cans chick-peas, rinsed and drained

1 onion, finely chopped

2–3 cloves garlic, finely chopped

2 tsps ground cumin,

¼ tsp chilli powder

2 tbsps chopped flat-leaf parsley

1 egg

2 tbsps flour

sea-salt flakes and freshly ground black pepper

vegetable oil, for frying

for the dip

250 ml natural yogurt

handful of mint

1 tbsp lemon juice

1 lemon, cut into wedges

When buying ready-cooked chick-peas, check that they are low in salt (or sodium, as salt is often referred to on food labels). It is also a good idea to rinse canned beans before using them. These are good with pitta bread and salad.

1 Put the chick-peas, onion, and garlic into a food processor or blender and whiz into a smooth paste.

2 Add the spices, parsley, and egg, and blend again.

3 Put the chick-pea mixture into a large bowl and add the flour and seasoning. Cover and leave to rest for 15 minutes to allow the flavours to develop and the flour to be absorbed.

4 Meanwhile, to make the sauce, put the yogurt into a bowl and stir in the mint and lemon juice. Cover and refrigerate.

5 Flour your hands lightly and mould the chickpea mixture into little rounds (about 12).

6 Heat some oil in a frying pan and cook the felafel until golden and crisp on both sides. Serve with the minty yogurt and lemon wedges.

fish with a crisp topping

makes: 4 servings or 2 servings plus 1–2 adult servings
also suitable for: over 8 months
nutrition: protein and zinc
storage: best eaten immediately

This is really quick and easy. When buying fresh fish, look for good, firm flesh and bright, shiny skin, scales, and eyes. Most smoked haddock is bright yellow because it has been artificially dyed, so choose organic smoked haddock, which will be pale yellow in colour with a much more subtle flavour.

75 g couscous
100 ml boiling weak vegetable stock
1 tbsp lemon juice
1 tbsp finely chopped parsley
freshly ground black pepper
4 pieces of hake, haddock or smoked haddock, skinned and boned
1 egg, beaten
olive oil, for greasing and drizzling

1 Preheat the oven to 190°C/ 375°F/gas mark 5.
2 Put the couscous into a heat-proof bowl. Pour in the stock. Cover and leave for 10 minutes.
3 Add the lemon juice and parsley, and season with pepper.
4 Dip the fish into the egg, then into the couscous to coat.

5 Arrange the coated fish on an oiled baking sheet, drizzle with a little extra oil, and bake for 15 to 20 minutes, until the topping is golden and crisp.

peppers with a cheesy filling

makes: 4 filled peppers
nutrition: protein and vitamin C
storage: 24 hours in the fridge

Brioche is a fabulous sweet, rich bread that makes wonderful crumbs. Alternatively, use day-old croissant or wholegrain bread. Stuffing vegetables is a great way to make them more interesting for children. Avoid green peppers, as they are too bitter.

2 orange peppers
2 yellow peppers
75 g brioche crumbs
25 g pine nuts, toasted and finely chopped (do not give nuts to toddlers if there is any family history of allergies)
handful of flat-leaf parsley
handful of mint
250 g haloumi cheese (or mozzarella)
zest of 1 lemon
a few black olives (optional)
2 tbsps extra virgin olive oil
sea-salt flakes and freshly ground black pepper

1 Preheat the oven to 190°C/ 375°F/gas mark 5.
2 Put the peppers, whole, into a roasting tin and roast for 45 minutes until soft. Remove from oven and leave to cool.
3 Put the brioche crumbs onto a baking sheet and toast in the oven for five minutes, turning the crumbs now and then until golden and crisp.

4 Remove from the oven and put into a bowl. Add the nuts, herbs, cheese, zest, olives, if using, and half the oil. Mix together and season to taste.
5 Slice the tops off the peppers and scoop out the seeds. Fill the peppers with the crumb mixture and drizzle with the remaining oil. Bake for 15 minutes, until warmed through.

lamb & papaya pilaf

makes: 5–6 servings or 2–3 servings plus 2 adult servings

nutrition: protein, fibre, iron, and betacarotene

storage: best served fresh (do not reheat rice)

400 g lamb chump steaks, cut into thin strips

4 tbsps olive oil

2 spring onions, finely chopped

2 cloves garlic, finely chopped

½ red chilli, deseeded and finely chopped

2 tsps freshly grated root ginger

2 lemon grass stalks, finely chopped

250 g wild rice mix

50 g currants or other organic dried fruit

pinch of ground coriander

pinch of ground cumin

700 ml weak low-salt vegetable stock

1 tbsp each of chopped fresh coriander and parsley

50 g flaked almonds, toasted and finely chopped (do not give nuts to toddlers if there is any family history of allergies)

2 papayas, halved, deseeded, peeled, and chopped into 1-cm cubes

for the marinade

1 tsp cumin seeds

1 tsp coriander seeds

1 tsp grated fresh root ginger

2 tsps honey

1 clove garlic, finely chopped

1 tbsp olive oil

This is a delicious meal for all the family.

1 Dry-fry the spices for the lamb marinade in a heavy-based frying pan for one to two minutes, then transfer to a bowl. Add the ginger, honey, garlic, and oil, and mix together. Add the lamb and rub all over, making sure that it is well coated. Cover and leave to marinate in the fridge for at least 30 minutes.

2 Heat half the oil in a large, heavy-based pan. Cook the spring onions over a low heat for about five minutes until soft but not brown.

3 Add the garlic, chilli, ginger, and lemon grass, and cook for two to three minutes.

4 Add the rice, dried fruit, coriander, and cumin. Pour in the stock. Stir well, then cover and cook for 30 minutes until all the liquid has been absorbed.

5 While the rice is cooking, heat a heavy-based frying pan. Add the remaining oil and cook the lamb pieces until well browned (this is best done in two batches).

6 Once the rice is cooked, check the seasoning, then add the herbs, almonds, lamb, and papaya. Stir to combine. Serve immediately.

treats

billy's baked apple meringue

makes: 6–8 servings

nutrition: vitamins B_{12} and C, protein, and iron

storage: best eaten fresh but can be eaten cold the next day; do not reheat meringue

5 large cooking apples, peeled, cored, and chopped

25 g unsalted butter

75 g golden caster sugar

2 eggs, separated

finely grated zest of 1 lemon

This is a very easy pudding, and kids love it: meringue always seems to be a favourite. You could add a few berries to the apple mixture to make it more colourful, but the lemon and apple combination is delicious. When using the zest of citrus fruit, you may wish to choose organic as most of the chemical residues in non-organic fruit are found in the skin.

1 Preheat the oven to 180°C/ 350°F/gas mark 4.

2 Put the apples in a saucepan with five tablespoons of water and cook over a gentle heat for about 15 minutes until soft.

3 Stir in the butter, one tablespoon of the sugar, the egg yolks, and lemon zest. Mix well.

4 Spoon into a lightly buttered ovenproof dish.

5 In a large bowl, whisk the egg whites until stiff. Gradually whisk in the remaining sugar and beat until the meringue stands up in peaks.

6 Spoon the meringue over the apples, using the spoon to make pointy peaks.

7 Cook for 15 to 20 minutes until the meringue is golden brown. Leave to cool slightly before serving

fruity ices

makes: 10 large ice cubes
nutrition: vitamin C
storage: up to 1 month in the freezer

125 g fruit of your choice, e.g. mango, papaya, banana, raspberries, strawberries, blueberries, blackberries, pineapple, or kiwi fruit

100 ml water or fruit juice

These are similar to yogurt ices but made with water or fruit juice, which is great if you are trying to avoid giving your child dairy products. You can make these into Slush Puppy-style drinks by whizzing the ice-cubes in a blender (or check that your food processor can cope with ice) with some water or fruit juice.

Purée the fruit of your choice with a hand-held blender or in a food processor or blender. Mix into the liquid. Pour into an ice-cube tray, cover, and freeze overnight.

homemade lemonade

makes: about 1.3 litres
nutrition: vitamin C
storage: up to 3 days in the fridge

4 lemons
75 g golden caster sugar
1.1 litres boiling water

This is very easy and much nicer than artificial, shop-bought lemon drinks. You may wish to use organic lemons to avoid chemical residues often found in the rind. If you find the lemonade is too strong, dilute with water to suit your toddler's taste. This drink is still best kept as an occasional treat, offering water as the main drink.

1 Remove the lemon zest with a sharp knife or potato peeler, being careful to avoid any of the bitter white pith.
2 Put the zest and sugar in a heat-proof bowl or jug and pour in the boiling water.
3 Cover and leave to cool, stirring occasionally. Meanwhile, squeeze the lemons and add the juice to the liquid.
4 Leave for at least an hour, then strain and serve.

fruity frozen yogurts

makes: 10 large ice-cubes

nutritional: vitamin C and calcium

storage: up to 1 month in the freezer

125g fruit of your choice, e.g. mango, papaya, banana, raspberries, strawberries, blueberries, blackberries, pineapple, or kiwi fruit

100 g natural yogurt or soya yogurt

These are a brilliant alternative to ice-cream. Buy fruit in season for a natural sweetness and a great flavour. These may be a little messy to eat, but it's much safer than using sticks for children of this age. Alternatively, freeze the mixture in egg cups. When it's slushy, put teaspoons in the middle and leave to freeze until hard. To turn them out, dip the egg cups in hot water for a moment or two.

1 Purée the fruit of your choice with a hand-held blender or in a food processor or blender.

2 Mix into the yogurt.

3 Pour into an ice-cube tray, cover, and freeze overnight.

cheesy rice krispie biscuits

makes: 12 biscuits

nutrition: protein and calcium

storage: 1 week in an airtight container or up to 3 months in the freezer

25 g Rice Krispies

50 g butter, softened

65 g plain flour, sieved

125 g Cheddar cheese, grated

pinch of cayenne pepper

These are delicious – you can use any hard cheese or a mixture of two or three cheeses such as Parmesan and Cheddar or Roquefort. The biscuits will keep well in a tin and can be frozen for up to three months. They are best warmed through before serving if they come from the freezer.

1 Preheat the oven to 190°C/ 375°F/gas mark 5.

2 Crush the cereal with a rolling pin in a plastic bag.

3 In a bowl, rub the butter into the flour. Stir in the cheese, cayenne, and cereal. Mix to a dough. Take spoonfuls of the mixture and roll into small balls. Arrange on a baking sheet and flatten with a fork.

4 Bake for about 10 minutes until golden, then leave to cool on a wire rack.

fruity flapjacks

makes: about 10

also suitable for: over 1 year if nuts and seeds are finely chopped

nutrition: fibre, calcium, potassium, magnesium, and carbohydrate

storage: 1 week in an airtight container or up to 3 months in the freezer

75 g unsalted butter

40 g honey

½ tsp bicarbonate of soda

250 g oats

25 g sunflower seeds, finely chopped

25 g nuts, finely chopped (optional)

2 ripe bananas, peeled and mashed

30 g dried fruit of your choice, e.g. sultanas, raisins, or apricots

This is another children's classic, but these flapjacks are made with honey rather refined sugar, which gives them a lovely flavour. Do not give nuts to toddlers if there is any family history of allergies.

1 Preheat the oven to 160°C/ 325°F/gas mark 3.
2 Lightly grease and line a 20-cm square tin.
3 Melt the butter and honey together in a saucepan.
4 Add the bicarbonate of soda and stir well. Add all the other ingredients and mix again.

5 Spoon into the tin and level out.
6 Bake for 15 to 20 minutes, until light golden.
7 Mark into squares, then leave to cool. Turn out onto a board and cut into squares.

cinnamon scones

makes: 12

also suitable for: over 10 months occasionally

nutrition: carbohydrate and protein

storage: 1 week in an airtight tin or up to 3 months in the freezer

200 g self-raising flour

½ tsp baking powder

½ tsp ground cinnamon

1 tbsp golden caster sugar

4 tbsps sour cream

1 egg, beaten

75 ml milk

These are not very sweet and are good served for breakfast as well, with fresh fruit. They freeze brilliantly. Try serving them warm with cream cheese.

1 Preheat the oven to 220°C/ 425°F/gas mark 7.
2 Sieve the flour, baking powder, and cinnamon into a bowl. Stir in the sugar, then make a well in the centre.
3 In a separate bowl, mix together the soured cream, egg, and milk, and pour into the dry ingredients. Mix together but do not beat.

4 Drop 10 teaspoonfuls of the mixture onto a lightly buttered baking sheet and bake for 12 to 14 minutes, until risen and golden. Serve warm if possible.

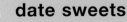

date sweets

makes: 6

nutrition: fibre, iron, and potassium

storage: 1 week in an airtight container in the fridge

20 g unsalted butter

6 fresh Medjool dates, stoned and chopped

2 ginger and cinnamon cookies, or other organic cookies

20 g tenderized or unsweetened desiccated coconut (do not give nuts to toddlers if there is any family history of allergies)

These make great sweet treats for kids, without the huge quantities of sugar and additives commonly found in ordinary confectionery. Fresh dates are very different from the sticky dried dates traditionally eaten at Christmas. Look out for fresh Medjool dates: they are plump and delicious.

1 Melt the butter in a saucepan and add the chopped dates.
2 Crush the biscuits into little pieces and add to the butter and date mixture.
3 Leave the mixture to cool a little, then roll into little balls and roll in the coconut.

butter-bean pâté

makes: 3–4 servings plus 1–2 adult servings

also suitable for: over 10 months in small quantities with bread

nutrition: protein

storage: 24 hours in the fridge

400 g can butter-beans, drained

3 tbsps olive oil

½ clove garlic, crushed (optional)

1 tbsp lemon juice

2 tbsps chopped fresh coriander or parsley, or 1 tbsp of each

pinch of paprika

freshly ground black pepper

bread, toast, or vegetable sticks, to serve

This is delicious served on nutty bread or toast, or with raw vegetables cut into sticks – try carrots, celery, and cucumber – and tomato wedges.

1 Whiz all the ingredients together with a hand-held blender or in a food processor or blender to a smooth purée. Season to taste with pepper.
2 Serve with bread, toast, or thin sticks of raw vegetables.

spiced apple cake with biscuit bottom

makes: 10 squares

nutrition: vitamin C, fibre, and energy

storage: 1 week in an airtight container or up to 3 months in the freezer

310 g self-raising flour

180 g unrefined, soft brown sugar

½ tsp allspice

½ tsp ground cinnamon

pinch of freshly grated nutmeg

115 g unsalted butter

1 tsp bicarbonate of soda

250 ml milk

1 egg, beaten

30 g dried apples, finely chopped

2 eating apples, cored and thinly sliced

This is a tasty cake with lots of different textures to interest children. It is delicious either served warm with yogurt or custard as a pudding or cold as a teatime treat. It freezes brilliantly and you can defrost the pieces as and when you need them.

There are many British-grown varieties of apple available; look for them at your local farmers' market if you get the chance. Alternatively, make this cake using dried and fresh pears and swap the cinnamon for ground ginger.

1 Preheat the oven to 180°C/ 350°F/gas mark 4.

2 In a bowl, sift the flour, sugar, allspice, cinnamon, and nutmeg together, then rub in the butter. Spread half the mixture into a greased 20-cm square cake tin. Pat it down evenly.

3 Dissolve the bicarbonate of soda in the milk. Add the beaten egg and chopped dried apple, and stir until combined. Pour over the remaining flour mixture and stir again until well combined.

4 Spread half the apple slices on top of the biscuit base. Pour in the sponge mixture, spread out evenly, then arrange the remaining apple slices on top. Bake in the oven for 45 minutes. Leave to cool slightly, then cut into squares.

banana & coconut cookies

makes: 15

nutrition: potassium, energy, and fibre

storage: 1 week in an airtight container

125 g unsalted butter

100 g golden caster sugar

1 egg

a few drops of vanilla extract

200 g self-raising flour

1 ripe banana, peeled and chopped

40 g unsweetened desiccated coconut

40 g dried banana chips

These lovely crunchy biscuits are great for children to chew on. It's very easy to make your own biscuits and they are much better health-wise, since they don't have all the additives and E-numbers of shop-bought ones. Do not give nuts to toddlers if there is any family history of allergies.

1 Preheat the oven to 180°C/350°F/gas mark 4.

2 In a bowl, beat the butter, sugar, egg, and vanilla together, or whiz together in a food processor or blender.

3 Sift in the flour and add the fresh banana and coconut. Mix together to form a soft dough.

4 Place teaspoons of the mixture onto a greased baking tray, leaving 5 cm between each. Top with the banana chips. Bake for 10 to 12 minutes until golden. Leave to cool on the tray.

fruit or mushrooms in bacon

makes: 20

nutrition: protein, fibre, iron, and potassium

storage: 24 hours in the fridge

20 prunes or ready-to-eat dried apricots or dried dates, stoned, or chestnut mushrooms, halved

10 rashers of unsmoked bacon

These are great for nibbling on or serving at a toddler's party.

1 Preheat the oven to 200°C/400°F/gas mark 6.

2 Cut each bacon rasher in half and wrap around a prune, apricot, date, or half a mushroom. Secure with a wooden cocktail stick.

3 Cook on a baking sheet for 35 to 40 minutes (whether you use mushrooms, prunes, apricots, or dates) until the bacon is crisp. If using fruit, leave to cool slightly before serving, since the fruit can get very hot.

piggies in a blanket

makes: 8

also suitable for: over 1 year

nutrition: protein and carbohydrate

storage: 2 days in the fridge or up to 2 months in the freezer

1 tbsp olive oil

1 leek, washed, trimmed, and finely chopped

50 g mushrooms, finely chopped

200 g sausage meat

1 tbsp chopped parsley

freshly ground black pepper

250 g ready-made puff pastry

milk, for sealing and brushing

These are quick and easy to prepare and are packed with flavour, making the perfect savoury treat.

1 Preheat the oven to 200°C/400°F/gas mark 6.

2 Heat the oil in a frying pan, add the leek and mushrooms, and sauté for a few minutes. Transfer to a bowl, leave to cool, then add the sausage meat, parsley, and pepper to taste. Mix everything together.

3 Roll out the pastry into a large rectangle. Place the sausage meat mixture in a long line down the centre. Moisten the edges with a little milk and roll together to make a long sausage. Turn it over so that the seam is along the bottom.

4 Slash the top and brush with milk, then cut into eight sausage rolls.

5 Place on a greased baking sheet and bake for 25 minutes.

lemon drizzle cakes

makes: 12

nutrition: carbohydrate and vitamin C

storage: 2 weeks in airtight tin or up to 3 months in the freezer

125 g butter

100 g golden caster sugar

2 eggs, beaten

125 g self-raising flour

finely grated zest and juice of 1 lemon

for the icing

finely grated zest and juice of ½ lemon

30 g golden icing sugar

Try to limit the times that you give your toddler anything sweet to very occasionally. These are best eaten while still slightly warm.

1 Preheat the oven to 190°C/375°F/gas mark 5.

2 In a bowl, cream together the butter and sugar. Add the eggs and sift in the flour. Add the lemon zest and juice, and mix everything together.

3 Put spoonfuls into paper cases and then into a muffin tray. Bake in the oven for 15 to 20 minutes until risen and golden.

4 While the cakes are cooking, mix together the lemon zest and juice and icing sugar.

5 When the cakes come out of the oven, drizzle the icing over them and leave to cool.

Good nutrition for babies and toddlers is fundamental to good health later in life. My "foods to avoid" guide, pages 132–3, will help you to broaden your child's diet safely. There are several organizations that provide professional advice on child nutrition and parenting issues – *see* "Useful Addresses", page 139, for details.

Buying fresh food is cheaper if you shop in season – *see* my chart on pages 134–5 for details. Remember to check out farmers' markets and farm shops in your area; produce from these sources is usually much cheaper and generally fresher.

Organic food is the fastest-growing area of food production. Standards can vary, so I have given a clear guide to organic certification and a glossary of label terms, so that you can choose foods that meet the highest standards. I have also included a chart comparing ready-made organic and non-organic baby foods (*see* pages 136–7).

baby
reference

foods
to avoid

Some foods need to be avoided when starting to wean babies, and should only be introduced when they reach certain ages. Read the introduction to each recipe section for more details. This list explains why these foods should be avoided.

Take particular care if there is a history of allergies in either parent's family. If you have any concerns, seek professional advice from your GP or a state-registered dietician or registered nutritionist. *See pages 34–5 for* information on immune-boosting foods and food allergies.

soft eggs

These may contain the food-poisoning bacteria salmonella, to which babies are more sensitive. Also, some small babies may react adversely to eggs, although generally the white is more likely to cause a reaction than the yolk. Small amounts of well-cooked egg can be given at seven months.

soft cheeses

These may contain the food-poisoning bacteria listeria, to which babies, again, are more sensitive.

nuts & seeds

This includes peanuts and nut spreads. These can cause a serious allergy in some children. Peanuts often cause the worst reactions, sometimes with fatal results. Research suggests that children most at risk are those in families with a history of allergy, particularly hayfever, asthma, eczema, or any food allergy. Under the age of three, these children should not consume any nuts or nut products. Other children can be given finely ground nuts or nut butters from seven months. Whole nuts and seeds are unsuitable for children under five because of the danger of choking.

cow's milk

This is unsuitable for babies under six months, since it is too high in salt and protein. From seven months, full fat cow's milk can be introduced gradually, but watch for any adverse reaction. Soya milks should be specially formulated for babies if they are used instead of breast milk and should be fortified if used as an alternative to cow's milk for babies and young children.

The advice about milk from the UK Department of Health is as follows: up until one year old, your baby needs 500 ml of breast milk or formula a day. Due to a lack of iron, cow's, sheep's, or goat's milk is not suitable as the main drink. However, after seven months of age, you can introduce cow's milk in small quantities in cooking, e.g. for making sauces. When your toddler is between the age of one and two years, full-fat milk can be given as a drink – not semi-skimmed or skimmed, because toddlers need the fat and vitamins that whole milk provides. From two years old, semi-skimmed milk can be introduced gradually as a main drink, providing the child is eating a varied diet supplying sufficient calories. Skimmed milk should only be given to children over five.

citrus fruits

These are too acidic for babies. The high sugar and fruit-acid content of citrus-fruit juices mean that they are a major cause of tooth decay. They should be diluted when given to toddlers as a drink.

salt

Salt should not be included in the diet of a baby under the age of one; the kidneys are immature and cannot process it. Salt can also cause dehydration, and a diet high in salt can lead to high blood pressure later in life. We need very little salt in our diets; there is enough found naturally in most foods to meet your child's needs. Particular foods to avoid are yeast extracts and stock cubes, both of which are often high in salt. Remember also that, on most food labels, salt is referred to as sodium. To convert sodium to salt, multiply the sodium figure by 2.5, i.e. 1 g of sodium per 100 g is the same as 2.5 g of salt.

honey

Honey may contain botulism spores, which can cause food poisoning. Babies cannot tolerate these spores. By the time they are walking, most toddlers have some resistance to them.

sugar

Sugar provides calories but few nutrients. Too much sugar is a cause of tooth decay and can lead to diabetes and obesity in later life. It is not necessary to add sugar to your child's food, except to sweeten naturally sour foods. Artificial sweetners can cause bloating, diarrhoea, wind, and other side-effects, and should never be given.

Check food labels carefully because sugar may be present as sucrose, glucose, fructose, lactose, hydrolyzed starch, invert sugar, and products such as treacle, honey, and golden syrup.

wheat, rye, oats, & barley

These and their derivatives (pasta, flour, bread, cereals, etc.) contain gluten, which can cause coeliac disease in a small number of babies if fed to them under the age of six months. Coeliac disease causes damage to the intestines, which means that nutrients cannot be absorbed properly. Once diagnosed, the sufferer can be prescribed a gluten-free diet.

tea & coffee

These contain tannins, which inhibit the absorption of iron, and should be avoided at all ages.

shellfish

Shellfish can trigger allergic reactions. Avoid until your child is at least two years old.

hot and spicy foods

Avoid excessively hot or spicy foods which can burn or inflame babies stomachs.

seasonal foods

	December	January	February	March	April	May
fruit						
apples	●	●	●	●	●	●
citrus fruit	●	●	●	●		
grapes	●	●				
pears	●	●	●			
rhubarb	●	●	●	●	●	●
beetroot	●	●	●			
vegetables						
broccoli				●	●	●
carrots		●	●	●	●	●
celery		●	●			
chard			●			
cucumbers				●	●	●
leeks				●	●	
mushrooms	●	●	●	●	●	●
onions	●	●	●			
parsnips	●	●	●			
potatoes	●	●	●	●	●	●
potatoes (new)						●
spinach					●	●
sweet potatoes	●	●	●			
fish						
cod	●	●	●			
haddock	●	●	●			
lemon sole	●	●	●			
salmon				●	●	●
meat						
lamb						●
turkey	●	●				

	June	July	August	September	October	November
fruit						
apples	●			●	●	●
apricots				●		
blackberries		●	●	●	●	
blueberries		●	●			
cherries	●	●	●			
peaches		●	●	●		
nectarines		●	●	●		
pears				●	●	●
plums			●			
raspberries	●	●	●	●	●	
rhubarb	●	●	●	●		●
strawberries	●	●	●	●	●	
vegetables						
asparagus	●					
aubergines				●	●	
beetroot	●	●	●	●	●	●
broad beans	●	●	●			
broccoli	●	●	●	●	●	●
carrots	●	●	●	●		
peppers				●	●	
cucumbers	●	●	●	●	●	
mushrooms	●	●	●	●	●	●
peas	●	●	●			
potatoes				●	●	●
potatoes (new)	●					
pumpkin			●	●	●	●
spinach	●	●	●	●	●	●
sweetcorn			●	●	●	
tomatoes		●	●	●		
watercress				●	●	●
fish						
cod				●	●	●
dover sole	●	●	●	●	●	●
haddock	●	●	●	●	●	●
halibut				●	●	●
meat	●	●	●			
lamb	●					
turkey						●

organic
food benefits

product	organic main ingredients	non-organic main ingredients
rusks	Wheat flour, raw cane sugar, sunflower and palm oils, soya flour, raising agents.	Wheat flour, sugar, vegetable oil, calcium carbonate, emulsifier, (glycerol monostearate), niacin, iron, thiamin, riboflavin, vitamin D.
bread sticks	Wheat flour, olive oil, yeast, malt.	Wheat flour, vegetable oil, malt extract, yeast, salt.
yogurts	**banana yogurt** Water, banana, thickeners (rice starch, maize starch).	**strawberry yogurt** Sugar, strawberry purée, glucose syrup, thickeners (pectin, guar gum).
packet cereals	**apple and banana muesli** Oat flakes, wheat flakes, apple flakes, banana flakes, maize flakes, dried apple pieces.	**fruity muesli** Apricots, flours (rice, oat, wheat), oat flakes, sugar, skimmed milk powder, vegetable oil, natural flavourings, calcium carbonate, vitamin C, calcium lactate, vitamin E, niacin, zinc, sulphate, iron, riboflavin, vitamin B_6, thiamine, vitamin A, folic acid, vitamin D, vitamin B_{12}.
porridge	**banana porridge** Banana purée (55%), water (33%), lemon juice (7%), oats (5%).	**apple & banana cereal** Apple juice (50%), apples (16%), bananas (14%), lemon juice, dried skimmed milk, oat flour, rice flour, wheat flakes, cornflour, vitamin C.
vegetable ready-made meals	**broccoli & cheese bake** Vegetables (potatoes, carrots, broccoli, onion – 50%), water, full-cream milk, cheese, ground rice.	**cheesy broccoli & potato bake** Potatoes (30%), skimmed milk, water, broccoli (11%), carrots, modified cornflour, cheese (1%), wheat flour, vegetable stock, onion powder, iron sulphate.
meat ready-made meals	**vegetables with noodles & chicken** Vegetables (tomatoes, carrots, peas, onions – 43%), water, noodles (21%), chicken (8%), wheat flour, corn oil.	**pasta shells with chicken and mushrooms** Pasta shells (27%), water, skimmed milk, chicken (8%), mushrooms (5%), cornflour, modified cornflour, cheese, vegetable oil, chicken stock, onion powder, herb extracts, sage extract, parsley, iron sulphate.

Some ready-made baby foods are essential for busy parents; many are now available in organic form. Here is my guide to the most useful.

nutrition	organic advantages	non-organic disadvantages
Wheat flour is high in B vitamins, fibre, zinc, and magnesium.	Organic wheat is richer in nutrients, so they are not added artificially.	Non-organic wheat is often treated with large amounts of chemicals, which can deplete the nutrient content.
This snack provides a good source of fibre from the wheat, and some B-complex vitamins.	Quality ingredients do not need salt to enhance their flavours.	Non-organic bread sticks are often high in salt.
Yogurt is a good protein provider and contains good levels of calcium and zinc.	Organic milk is used, which is free from chemical residues.	The milk used to make the yogurt may contain residues, e.g. antibiotics.
Oats provide vitamins as well as potassium and calcium. Wheat is a good source of fibre. Bananas also provide fibre, potassium, and magnesium. Apples contain pectin, potassium, and vitamin C. Apricots are a good source of iron, potassium, and betacarotene.	Quality ingredients are full of natural nutrients.	Large amounts of chemicals are very often used in the harvesting of nearly all non-organic cereals, which can reduce their nutrient content, so nutrients are often added later.
Bananas contain high levels of potassium and are a good source of soluble fibre and magnesium. Apples contain good levels of pectin, vitamin C, and potassium.	Organic fruit is left to ripen naturally, so it has a better flavour and higher nutrient content.	Bananas and apples are very often heavily sprayed with insecticides, and residues can be found in the fruit.
Potatoes are a great source of protein, vitamin C, and other B vitamins. The broccoli is also rich in vitamin C, as well as vitamin A, folic acid, iron, and potassium.	Organic potatoes have a much better flavour and higher nutrient content.	Non-organic potatoes are frequently sprayed with a variety of insecticides and other chemicals.
The organic meal is made up of 43% vegetables – all important to a healthy, balanced diet, providing vitamins and minerals. The chicken in both dishes is protein-rich and the noodles/pasta provide carbohydrates.	Vegetables grown organically are often nutritionally superior. Organic chickens are given natural feed, which gives the meat a much better flavour and avoids the risk of ingesting growth hormones.	Non-organic chickens are routinely given antibiotics and feed made from fish meal, which can affect their flavour.

organic certification

In the UK, the government has created the UK Register of Organic Food Standards (UKROFS), which approves organic food-inspection bodies (*see* table, right). These organizations ensure that farmers wishing to produce and sell organic products are thoroughly inspected and continue to maintain the high standards required. Once a farm has been approved, which means that a farmer has conformed to a set of guidelines on the production and processing of organic produce, it can label its produce with a certification symbol. Check the label to make sure that it carries one of these symbols.

The most widespread approved symbol in the UK is that of the Soil Association, which covers around 70 to 80 per cent of all certified organic food on sale in the UK.

The table gives details of the various organic food inspection bodies approved by the UK Register of Organic Food Standards. If organic products are imported, EU regulations demand that they are inspected, approved, and thus certified by one of these bodies to the same standards as those applied in the UK and the rest of the EU.

Several bodies exist to regulate organic production and processing systems around the world, so that what is considered organic in one country meets the standards of inspection in another.

guarantees and certification register

The Soil Association
Bristol House, 40–56 Victoria Street,
Bristol BS1 6BY
Tel: 0117 929 0661

The Biodynamic Agricultural Association (BDAA)
Painswick Inn,
Stroud, Gloucestershire, GL5 1QG
Tel: 01453 759501

The Irish Organic Farmers and Growers Association
Harbour Building, Harbour Road,
Kilbeggan, County Westmeath, Ireland
Tel: 00 353 506 32563

Organic Farmers and Growers
The Elim Centre, Lancaster Road,
Shrewsbury, Shropshire SY1 8LE
Tel: 01743 440512

The Scottish Organic Producers Association
Scottish Organic Centre, 10th Avenue,
Royal Highlands Centre, Ingliston, Edinburgh, EH28 8NF
Tel: 0131 335 6606

Organic Food Federation (OFF)
31 Turbine Way, Eco Tech Business Park,
Swaffham, Norfolk PE37 7XD
Tel: 01760 720444

UKROFS (UK Register of Organic Food Standards), Ministry of Agriculture, Fisheries and Food, Noble House, 17 Smith Square, London SW1P 3JR Tel: 020 7238 5605

The Vegetarian Society
Parkdale, Dunham Road
Altrincham
Cheshire WA14 4QG
Tel: 0161 925 2000
www.vegsoc.org

Vegan Society
Donald Watson House
7 Battle Road
St Leonard's on Sea
East Sussex TN37 7AA
Tel: 01424 427393
www.vegansociety.com

**La Leche League
Great Britain**
PO Box 29, West Bridgford
Nottingham NG2 7NP
Tel: 0845 120 2918
www.laleche.org.uk
*Provides breast-feeding advice and
support*

National Childbirth Trust
Alexandra House, Oldham Terrace
London W3 6NH
Tel: 0870 770 3236
www.nctpregnancyandbabycare.com
*Provides support during pregnancy,
childbirth, and
early parenthood*

**Association of Breast-feeding
Mothers**
ABM PO Box 207
Bridgewater
Somerset TA6 7YT
Tel: 020 7813 1481
www.abm.me.uk

**The Hyperactive Children's
Support Group**
71 Whyke Lane
Chichester
West Sussex PO19 7PD
Tel: 01243 551313
www.hacsg.org.uk

British Allergy Foundation
Deepdene House
30 Bellegrove Road
Welling
Kent DA16 3PY
Tel: 020 8303 8525
www.allergyfoundation.com

useful
addresses

fairtrade

Oxfam states: "Fairtrade aims to reduce poverty in developing nations by helping poorer producers to help themselves. It is not about charity. It is about paying Third World producers a fair price and helping them gain access to UK markets."

Under the Fairtrade agreement, Third World workers and producers are protected by:
- fairer wages and better working and living conditions, including clean water, education, and medical aid;
- minimal exposure to high levels of pesticides and chemicals;
- improved terms of trade; and
- secure long-term contracts.

biodynamic

"Biodynamic" agriculture is based on the principles of the Austrian philosopher Rudolf Steiner. Planting and other farm activities follow a calendar based on the movement of the moon, the planets, and the stars, and involve the use of special natural soil and plant preparations. The farms aim to be self-sustaining ecosystems. The certifying body, Demeter, is an internationally approved organization, like the Soil Association. All biodynamic foods are 100 per cent organic.

transitional products

British suppliers cannot meet the demand for organic foods in this country. As a result, 70 per cent of organic foods are imported. One of the reasons why we cannot keep

label terms

up with demand is the length of time it takes for a farmer to convert to organic farming methods.

A non-organic farmer converting to organic will endure a two-year conversion period before being approved for certification. This period allows the soil to rebuild its natural fertility and pesticide residues to be reduced.

To help the farmers during this expensive period, some supermarkets, e.g. Waitrose, have started to sell "transitional products". This is produce from farms that are in the process of converting. It allows consumers the option to choose foods that should be lower in residues than their non-organic equivalents and it helps to support the farmers who can charge slightly higher prices for their goods, which in turn helps them to cope with the cost of transfer to an organic way of farming.

index

For Olivia, Pia, and William, my godchildren

I would like to thank everyone who has helped me put this book together.

In particular, Becca for giving me the opportunity to write this book and to Phil, Miranda, and Bill for making the book look so fantastic. A big 'thank you' goes to Billy and Alison Blackwell for their tireless help with the research, to Fiona for assisting with recipe testing, and to Tanya for her invaluable comments on nutrition. I should also like to thank the Soil Association, Catherine at La Leche League, and the National Childbirth Trust for all their advice.

Finally, as always, thank you to David, Pop, and Vicki for their continued support.